PANCE/PANRE Study Guide
Physician Assistant Board Review

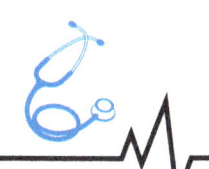

Lauren Russo
Adam Roth

TABLE OF CONTENTS

MUSCULOSKELETAL	2
GASTROINTESTINAL	12
EAR EYE NOSE THROAT	24
PULMONARY	34
CARDIOVASCULAR SYSTEM	42
HEMATOLOGY AND ONCOLOGY	53
INFECTIOUS DISEASE	58
GENITOURINARY	65
NEUROLOGY	72
ENDOCRINE	80
DERMATOLOGY	86
PSYCHIATRY	94
REPRODUCTIVE	99
HEALTH MAINTENANCE	109

MUSCULOSKELETAL

ROTATOR CUFF INJURY

1. Muscles in rotator cuff: Supraspinatus, subscapularis, infraspinatus, teres minor
2. Rotator cuff inflammation:
   - Neer's test:
     * Forward arm flexion, press greater tuberosity and supraspinatus muscle.
     * Positive test is pain
   - Hawkins test:
     * Abduct shoulder 90 degree, flex elbow 90, rotate arm to limit.
     * Positive test is pain
3. Supraspinatus tear or inflammation:
   - Empty can test:
     * 90 degree abduct, 30 degree flex, rotate internal. Apply downward pressure.
     * Positive test is weakness or pain
   - Full can test:
     * 90 degree abduct, 30 degree flex, rotate external. Apply downward pressure.
     * Positive test is weakness or pain
   - Arm drop:
     * Arm passively abducted and actively adducted slowly
     * Positive test is when arm drops quickly at 30 degrees
4. Subscapularis tear or inflammation:
   - Lift off test:
     * Elbow 90 degree, rotate medially against resistance.
     * Positive test is pain or weakness
5. Teres minor/infraspinatus tear or inflammation:
   - Elbow 90 degree, rotate laterally against resistance.
   - Positive test is pain or weakness

BICEPS TENDONITIS

1. Yergason's test:
   - Elbow flexed 90 degrees, wrist supinates against resistance
   - Positive test: Pain reproduced

SHOULDER DISLOCATION

1. MOI: fall on outstretched arm. (full abduction and extension)
2. Anterior dislocation more common.
3. Rule out axillary nerve, musculocutaneous nerve, brachial plexus, axillary artery injury
   - Axillary nerve: C5-C6 fibers. Motor: deltoid, teres minor, triceps. Sensation: shoulder joint, inferior deltoid
   - Musculocutaneous nerve: C5-C7 fibers. Motor: coracobrachialis, biceps, brachialis. Sensory: radial side forearm. Decreased biceps reflex
4. Treatment:
   - Reduce, postreduction films, sling and swath, physical therapy

MUSCULOSKELETAL

4. Tear of glenoid labrum: Bankart's lesion

AC JOINT SEPARATIONS

1. Tearing for acromioclavicular and/or coracoclavicular joints.
2. Presentation: Step off deformity
   → MOI: Fall on shoulder or impact to tip of shoulder.
3. Radiograph: AP view both shoulders.
4. Treatment: Conservative or surgical.

FRACTURED CLAVICLE

1. Most common fracture in children and adolescents
2. Presenation: Tenting of skin over clavicle
   → MOI: fall on outstretched arm
3. Rule out: Brachial plexus injury.
4. Treatment: Figure of 8 sling for 4-6 weeks.

HUMERAL SHAFT INJURY

1. Rule out radial nerve injury.
   → Radial nerve: C5-T1 fibers. Motor: triceps, hand extensors. Sensation: dorsal hand.

BOXER'S FRACTURE

1. Fracture of metacarpal neck of 4th or 5th finger.
2. MOI: Occurs from punching object. Often associated with alcohol.
3. Treatment:
   → Deformity of >40 degrees requires closed reduction.
   → Ulnar splint
   → Antibiotics if there is anopen wound (Ie. Cephalexin, Cefazolin)

COLLE'S FRACTURE

1. Distal radial fracture with dorsal angulation.
2. Dinnerfork deformity
3. MOI: Fall on extended hand

SMITH'S FRACTURE

1. Distal radial fracture with volvar angulation
2. Reverse dinner fork deformity

GAMEKEEPER'S THUMB

1. Sprain of Ulnar collateral ligament of the thumb.
2. Treatment:
   → Surgical correction for complete tear
   → Thumb spica splint for partial tear.

PANCE/PANRE Study Guide

MUSCULOSKELETAL

MEDIAL EPICONDYLITIS (GOLFER'S ELBOW)
1. MOI: Repeated flexion and pronation of wrist

LATERAL EPICONDYLITIS (TENNIS ELBOW)
1. Most common overuse injury of elbow
2. MOI: Repeated wrist extension

SCAPHOID (NAVICULAR) FRACTURE
1. Pain over anatomical snuff box (between extensor pollicis longus and brevis)
2. Blood supply from radial artery. Proximal pole has poor blood supply. May lead to avascular necrosis.
3. Radiograph:
   → AP, lateral, scaphoid view.
   → Avascular necrosis shows ground glass appearance.
4. Treatment:
   → Long-arm thumb spica.
   → Displacement >1mm requires ORIF
   → If radiograph is negative, repeat films in 2-3 weeks to rule out avascular necrosis

TRIGGER FINGER
1. Presentation:
   → Difficulty extending finger, audible snap and pain
   → Nodule in flexor tendon retinaculum

deQUERVIAN'S TENOSYNOVITIS
1. Stenosing tenosynovitis of abductor pollicis longus and extensor pollicis brevis
2. Positive Finkelstein's test - hand in fist with ulnar deviation reproduces pain

RADIAL HEAD FRACTURE
1. Radiograph: Anterior/posterior fat pad due to hemarthrosis
2. MOI: Fall on outstretched hand

ANKYLOSING SPONDYLITIS
1. Starts at SI joint and ascends
2. HLA-B27 positive
3. Radiology: Bamboo Spine (squaring of vertebral bodies with spine ossification and syndesmophytes)

SCOLIOSIS
1. Almost always right thoracic curves.
2. Treatment:
   → >30 degrees may need brace or surgery
   → Risser score of 3 or higher is less likely to progress.

MUSCULOSKELETAL

SPINAL STENOSIS
1. Presentation: Age 60+, pain relieved by leaning forward and aggrevated by walking
2. Thickened ligamentum flavum

KYPHOSIS
1. Curves >60 degrees may need Milwaukee brace or surgery
1. Juvenille Kyphosis is also known as Scheuermann's disease

KNEE/ANKLE ASSESSMENT
1. Ballottement:
    - Testing: Fluid/effusion in knee
    - Procedure: Press on knee cap
    - Positive test is patella floatation
2. McMurray:
    - Testing: Medial and Lateral Meniscus tear
    - Procedure: Flex knee, hold foot and knee, rotate medially (for lateral meniscus tear) or laterally (for medial meniscus tear) and extend knee.
    - Positive test is pain, clicking or limitation.
3. Apley Test:
    - Testing: Meniscus tear
    - Procedure: Patient prone, knee bent, tibia is compressed to knee while externally rotated.
    - Positive test is pain.
4. Drawer sign:
    - Testing: ACL and PCL tear
    - Procedure: Knee bent, pull tibia forward and backwards
    - Positive test is >5mm laxity.
5. Lachman test:
    - Testing: ACL
    - Knee is bent 10 degrees and pulled anteriorly
    - Positive test is >5 mm laxity.
6. Thompson test:
    - Testing: Achille's tendon rupture.
    - Squeeze calf
    - Positive test is absence of plantar flexion.

ANTERIOR CRUCIATE LIGAMENT TEAR
1. More common than PCL.
2. Presentation: Pop heard. Hemarthrosis 3-4 hrs. Knee instability.
    - MOI: Pivoting motion (running, jumping)
    - More common in females
3. Exam Findings: Lachman test (best) and Drawer sign positive
4. Treatment:
    - Surgical reconstruction if <40 years old or active
    - Nonoperative for less active patients

MUSCULOSKELETAL

MENISCAL TEAR

1. Medial meniscus injury is more common than lateral meniscus injury
2. Presentation: Joint line pain. Locking and giving way. Gradual swelling. Difficulty with stairs.
   → MOI: Excessive rotational force on femur.
3. Physical exam: McMurray (best) or Apley test.
4. "Unhappy triad"- Blow to lateral knee results in tear of ACL, MCL and medial meniscus

OSGOOD SCHLATTER

1. Apophysitis of tibial tubercle.
2. Presentation: Males 8-15 who play sports, painful lump below kneecap
   → MOI: Trauma or overuse
3. Treatment: Self limiting when epiphysis closes.

ANKLE SPRAIN

1. Anterior Talo-fibular ligament:
   → Most common
   → Lateral ankle
   → MOI: Ankle inversion during plantar flexion
2. Deltoid ligament:
   → Medial ankle
   → MOI: External rotational force

HIP FRACTURE

1. Femoral head and neck fracture presentation: External rotation and shortening of affected leg
   → Occurs after fall in elderly patients with osteoporosis
2. Treatment: ORIF within 48 hours for best results
3. Complications: Avascular necrosis

AVASCULAR NECROSIS OF THE HIP

1. Called "Leg Calve Perthes" in children
2. Dull ache, antalgic limp.
3. Radiograph of hip: Crescent sign
4. Treatment:
   → Initially: Protected weight bearing. Alendronate.
   → Definitive treatment: Total hip replacement

SLIPPED CAPITAL FEMORAL EPIPHYSIS

1. Weakened epiphyseal plate of femur. Displaced femoral head.
2. Classic patient: Male, 10-16 years old, African American, obese
3. Radiograph:

MUSCULOSKELETAL

- → Best seen in frog leg lateral pelvis or lateral hip view
- → "Melting ice cream cone"

4. Treatment: pinning in situ, nonweight bearing

CONGENITAL HIP DYSPLASIA

1. Barlow test – hip adduction causes dislocation
2. Ortolani test/sign – hip flexion and abduction with anterior pressure causes reduction of hip dislocation (CLICK auscultated)

TYPES OF FRACTURES

1. Transverse: Right angle to bone axis
2. Spiral/torsion: Bone has twist appearance
3. Oblique: Break is diagonal
4. Comminuted: Crushed
5. Segmental: In several large pieces
6. Angulation: Deviation from straight
7. Displacement: Abnormal position of fragments
8. Open fracture: Skin broken
9. Closed fracture: Skin intact
10. Dislocation: Bone displaced from joint.
11. Greenstick Fracture: fracture in long bone, Force to one side. bowing causes break in one side of cortex.
12. Torus (buckle) fracture: Compressive force. Break to one or two sides of cortex.

SALTER-HARRIS FRACTURE

1. SALTR
   - → Type I: Straight across (physis break)
   - → Type II: Above (metaphysis and physis break)
   - → Type III: Lower (epiphysis and physis break)
   - → Type IV: Through (metaphysis, epiphysis and physis break)
   - → Type V: Ruined (compression fracture, metaphysis, epiphysis and physis break)

OSTEOMYELITIS

1. Most often Staphylococcus aureus.
   - → Patients with sickle cell: Salmonella spp.
2. Treatment:
   - → Surgical debridement
   - → IV antibiotics- Empiric therapy (vancomycin + ciprofloxacin or ceftazidime or cefepime)
     - ✽ Pending cultures and sensitivities

MUCOUS CYSTS:

1. DIP joint. Originate from Heberden nodules

MUSCULOSKELETAL

GANGLION CYSTS
1. Located on dorsum of hand. Will transilluminate

ENCHONDROMA
1. Tumor of cartilage
2. Common, benign and asymptomatic
3. Location: often in hand

EWING'S SARCOMA
1. Malignant. Diaphysis of long bones, ribs and flat bones
2. Age range: 5-25 years old
3. Radiograph: "Onion skin appearance" of bone

OSTEOSARCOMA
1. Malignant. Metaphysis of long bones
2. Age range: 10-20 years old
3. Radiograph: "Sunburst on bone

BASILAR SKULL FRACTURE
1. Presentation: Raccoon eyes, battle sign, CSF rhinorrhea

PSORIATIC ARTHRITIS
1. Presentation: Sausage finger appearance
2. Radiograph: "Cup and saucer" or "pencil in cup" appearance of proximal phalanx

OSTEOARTHRITIS
1. Presentation:
    → Bouchard's nodes (PIP joints)
    → Heberden nodes (DIP joints)
    → Weight bearing joints
2. Joint fluid analysis:
    → Clear fluid, <2,000 leukocytes, <25% neutrophils, no organisms

RHEUMATOID ARTHRITIS
1. Presentation:
    → Females near age 40
    → Swan neck deformity. Joint inflammation visible. 3+ symmetrical joints. Morning stiffness >30 mins. Fatigue.
    → DIP joint usually spared.
2. Antibodies: Rheumatoid factor, anti-CCP
3. Joint Fluid analysis:
    → Yellow to white fluid, 2,000-50,000 leukocytes, 50% neutrophils, no organisms

MUSCULOSKELETAL

3. Treatment: DMARDS. Methotrexate is usually first. (Contraindicated in pregnancy)

JUVENILE RHEUMATOID ARTHRITIS

1. Population: Less than 16 years of age
3. Systemic JRA is Still's disease
   → Symptoms: Evening fever spikes, salmon pink macular papular rash and Koebner's phenomenon

GOUT

1. Presentation: Inflammatory joint pain. Great toe is often first affected
2. Associated with alcohol use, lunch meats and diuretic use
3. Joint fluid analysis: rod-shaped, negatively birefringent urate crystals
4. Treatment:
   → Acute- indomethacin
   → Chronic- allopurinol

PSEUDOGOUT

1. Presentation: Inflammatory joint pain, often associated with hyperparathryoidism
2. Joint fluid analysis: Rhomboid-shaped calcium pyrophosphate crystals, positive birefringent
3. Treatment: NSAIDs

REACTIVE ARTHRITIS (REITER'S SYNDROME)

1. Presentation: Classic tetrad- Urethritis, conjunctivitis, oligoarthritis, mucosal ulcers
   → Can't see, can't pee, can't climb a tree
2. After recent infection with Gonorrhea, Chlamydia, Shigella, Salmonella, Yersinia, or Campylobacter
3. HLA-B27 positive

SEPTIC ARTHRITIS

1. Organism: Most often S. aureus, in sexually active young adults consider N. gonorrhoeae
2. Joint fluid analysis:
   → Purulent fluid, >50,000 leukocytes, >75% neutrophils, organism present
3. Treatment: Joint drainage AND IV antibiotics:
   → Healthy patients: Vancomycin
   → IV drug users and sick patients: Vancomycin + ciprofloxacin or anti pseudomonal beta-lactam (ie. Ceftriaxone)

SYSTEMIC LUPUS ERYTHEMATOSUS

1. "SOAP BRAIN MD"
   → Serositis, Oral ulcers, Arthritis, Photosensitivity, Blood disorders, Renal involvement, Antinuclear antibodies, Immunologic phenomenon, Neurological disorder, Malar rash, Discoid rash
2. Antibodies: anti dsDNA (best test), ANA, anti Smith
3. Treatment: Hydroxychloroquine or quinacrine

MUSCULOSKELETAL

POLYMYOSITIS

1. Presentation: Pain and stiffness in proximal limbs, neck, pharynx
2. Associated with malignancy
3. Diagnostic studies:
   → Definitive: Muscle biopsy showing inflammation
   → Anti-Jo antibodies
4. Treatment: Steroids, methotrexate, azathioprine
5. Dermatomyositis:
   → Gotton's papules (scale/papules on dorsal hand), Shawl sign, Heliotrope rash (pink/purple rash around eyes)

POLYMYALGIA RHEUMATICA

1. Presentation: Pelvic girdle and shoulder pain. Severe after rest.
2. Associated with temporal arteritis
3. ESR: >50 mm/hr
4. Treatment: Steroid taper for 2 years

POLYARTERITIS NODOSA

1. Small and medium arteries
2. Associated with Hepatitis B
3. Presentation: Livedo reticularis and palpable purpura
4. Diagnostic studies: ANCA positive, and definitive diagnosis with vessel biopsy

SCLERODERMA

1. CREST: Calcinosis, Raynaud's phenomenon, Esophageal dysfunction (GERD), Sclerodactyly, telangiectgasis
2. Antibodies: Anti-centromere (limited) and anti-topoisomerase (systemic)
3. Treatment: Symptomatic

SJOGREN

1. Dry mucous membranes
2. Diagnosis:
   → Schirmer's tear test- Positive if < 5 mm lacrimation in 5 minutes
   → Anti-Ro and Anti-La antibodies
3. Treatment: Symptomatic

FIBROMYALGIA

1. Diagnosis of exclusion
2. Treatment: Pregabalin (Lyrica)

OSTEOPOROSIS

1. First line treatment: Bisphosphonates
2. DEXA:

MUSCULOSKELETAL

- T score- standard
    - Osteopenia: -1.0 to -2.5
    - Osteoporosis: <-2.5
- Z score- same age/gender
    - <-2.0: search underlying cause

CAUDA EQUINA

1. Presentation: Saddle anesthesia, loss of bowel/bladder function
2. Must rule this out when patients present with back pain or trauma

COMPARTMENT SYNDROME

1. 6 P's: Pain out of proportion, paresthesias, pallor, paralysis, pulselessness, poikilothermia (limb unable to regulate temp)
2. Treatment:
    - Acute: Fasciotomy- medial and lateral incisions
    - Chronic: Conservative or fasciotomy

SCIATICA

1. Distribution: Buttocks, posterior thigh, posterolateral aspect of leg, lateral malleolus and entire sole of foot
2. Causes: Disc herniation, piriformis muscle spasm, spinal stenosis, spondylolisthesis

OSTEOMALACIA

1. Radiograph: Pseudofractures (milkman lines or looser zones)

SPONDYLOLYSIS

1. Pars articularis fracture
2. Radiograph: Scotty Dog on spine
3. Complication: Spondylolisthesis (vertebra has slipped)

GASTROINTESTINAL

GASTROESOPHAGEAL REFLUX DISEASE

1. Clinical diagnosis
   → Indigestion worse with carbonation, greasy foods, spicy foods and laying down
2. Treatment: H2 receptor blockers, proton pump inhibitors, diet modification
3. Complications: Strictures or Barrett's esophagus

ESOPHAGITIS

1. Infectious
   → Rare unless immunocompromised
   → Organisms:
      * Candida- observe oral candidiasis in mouth, treat with fluconazole or ketoconazole
      * CMV- deep ulcers on EGD, treat with ganciclovir
      * HSV- shallow ulcers noted on EGD, treat with acyclovir
2. Pill induced
   → Most often: NSAIDs, Tetracyclines, Bisphosphonates
   → Treatment: Discontinue offending agent
3. GERD
   → Treatment: H2 receptor blockers, PPIs, diet modification

ACHALASIA

1. Decreased peristalsis, increased sphincter tone
2. Presentation: Slowly progressive dysphagia, episodic regurgitation
3. Diagnosis:
   → Barium swallow: "parrot-beak" - dilated esophagus tapered to distal obstruction
   → Definitive diagnosis: esophageal manometry

ZENKER'S DIVERTICULUM

1. Outpouching of posterior hypopharynx
2. Presentation:
   → Men over 60.
   → Regurgitant symptoms several hours after eating, halitosis
3. Treatment: Excision, myotomy of cricopharygneus muscle and upper 3 cm of posterior esophageal wall.

NEUROGENIC DYSPHAGIA

1. Dysphagia for liquids and solids.
2. Injury at brainstem or cranial nerves.

ESOPHAGEAL SPASM

1. Barium swallow: Corkscrew esophagus

GASTROINTESTINAL

ESOPHAGEAL CANCER

1. Adenocarcinoma:
   → Associated with Barrett's esophagitis
   → Lower 1/3rd of esophagus
2. Squamous cell:
   → Associated with smoking and alcohol use
   → Upper 2/3rds of esophagus
3. Progressive dysphagia, weight loss, hoarseness
4. Diagnostic studies: Endoscopy + biopsy
5. Treatment: Resection

MALLORY-WEISS TEAR

1. Esophageal mucosal tear
2. Presentation: Hematemesis
   → Caused by forceful vomiting. Associated with alcohol use
3. Treatment: Supportive. May cauterize or inject Epinephrine if needed.

BOERHAAVE SYNDROME

1. Rupture of esophageal wall.
2. Etiology: Iatrogenic (endoscope), caustic ingestion, pill esophagitis, barrett's, ulcers, esophageal strictures
3. Fatal without surgical correction

ESOPHAGEAL VARICES

1. Asymptomatic until hematemesis
2. Etiology: Portal hypertension (from cirrhosis), Budd-Chiari syndrome (from occlusion of hepatic veins)
3. Treatment:
   → Therapeutic endoscopy – banding or sclerotherapy
   → Prevent with beta blocker
   → Acutely treat with Octreotide

SPLENIC RUPTURE

1. Kehr sign - referred pain from spleen to left shoulder

GASTRITIS

1. Causes:
   → Autoimmune (pernicious anemia)
      * Location: Body of fundus.
   → H. pylori infection
      * Location: Antrum and body
      * Studies: Urea breath test or fecal antigen.
      * Treatment: PPI (Ie. Omeprazole) + clarithromycin + amoxicillin +/- metronidazole
   → NSAIDs, alcohol

PANCE/PANRE Study Guide

GASTROINTESTINAL

PEPTIC ULCER DISEASE

1. Etiology: H. pylori (most common), NSAID use, Zollinger-Ellison syndrome (refractory PUD)
2. Types:
   - Duodenal ulcer- pain improves with food
   - Gastric ulcer- pain worsens with food
3. Diagnosis: Endoscopy
4. Treatment:
   - H. pylori infection: PPI (Ie. Omeprazole) + clarithromycin + amoxicillin +/- metronidazole
   - NSAIDs use: discontinue use
   - Zollinger-Ellison syndrome: PPI and resect tumor

PYLORIC STENOSIS

1. Presentation:
   - 4-6 weeks of age with projectile vomiting
   - Olive-shaped mass on abdominal palpation
2. Barium swallow: string sign
3. Treatment: surgical correction

CHOLECYSTITIS

1. Presentation:
   - 5 Fs: Female, Fat, Forty, Fertile, Fair
   - RUQ pain after high fat meal
   - Murphy sign: Palpation of RUQ inhibits respiration
2. Diagnosis:
   - Ultrasound is the preferred initial imaging
     * Gallbladder wall >3 mm, pericholecystic fluid, gall stones
   - HIDA is the best test
3. Treatment: Cholecystectomy

CHOLANGITIS

1. Organsims: E. coli, Enterococcus, Klebsiella, Enterobacter
2. Presentation:
   - Charcot's triad: RUQ tenderness, jaundice, fever
   - Reynold's pentad: Charcot's triad + altered mental status and hypotension
3. Diagnostic studies:
   - Initial imaging: Ultrasound
   - Best: ERCP
4. Treatment:
   - Antibiotics, fluids and analgesia.
   - ERCP to remove stones, insert stent, repair sphincter
   - Cholecystectomy (performed post-acute)

GASTROINTESTINAL

PRIMARY SCLEROSING CHOLANGITIS

1. Jaundice and pruritus
2. Associated with IBD, cholangiocarcinoma, pancreatic cancer, colorectal cancer

VIRAL HEPATITIS

1. Symptoms: Tea colored urine, vague abdominal discomfort, nausea, pruritus, pale stool
2. Hepatitis A
   → Acute
   → Transmission: Fecal-oral
3. Hepatitis B
   → Acute and Chronic
   → Transmission: Sexual or sanguineous
   → Serology:
      * HBeAg – highly infectious
      * HBsAg – ongoing infection
      * Anti-HBc – had/have infection
         • IgM – acute
         • IgG – not acute
      * Anti-HBs – immune
   → Risk of hepatocellular carcinoma
4. Hepatitis C
   → Chronic
   → Asymptomatic
   → Transmission: IV drug use is most common. Also sexual or sanguineous
   → Risk of cirrhosis and hepatocellular carcinoma
5. Hepatitis D
   → Only occurs when coinfected with Hepatitis B
   → Risk of hepatocellular carcinoma
6. Hepatitis E
   → Pregnant woman, 3rd world countries
7. Treatment: Supportive. Vaccinate against other viral hepatitis. HIV treatment PRN.
   → Hepatitis C- Pegylated interferon and ribavirin

TOXIC HEPATITIS

1. Acetaminophen toxicity: Treatment with N-Acetylcysteine within 8-10 hrs

FATTY LIVER DISEASE

→ Risk factors: Obesity, hyperlipidemia, insulin resistance
→ Liver enzymes: ALT > AST
→ Liver biopsy: Large fat droplets (macro vesicular fatty infiltrates)

ALCOHOLIC HEPATITIS

1. Liver enzymes: AST:ALT ratio > 2:1

GASTROINTESTINAL

CIRRHOSIS

1. Presentation:
    - Ascites, pulmonary edema/effusion, esophageal varices, Terry's nails (white nail beds)
    - Hepatic encephalopathy:
        * Asterixis (flapping tremor), dysarthria, delirium, coma
2. Treatment: Avoid alcohol, restrict salt, transplant

HEPATOCELLULAR CARCINOMA

1. Etiology: Cirrhosis, Hepatitis B, Hepatitis C, Hepatitis D, Aflatoxin from aspergillus
2. Tumor Marker: Alpha-fetoprotein
3. Treatment: Resect, Transplant
4. Poor prognosis

ACUTE PANCREATITIS

1. Etiology: Cholelithiasis or alcohol abuse
2. Diagnosis:
    - Clinical + elevated lipase and amylase.
    - CT required to differentiate from necrotic pancreatitis
3. Signs: Grey turners (flank bruising), Cullen's sign (bruising near umbilicus)
4. Ranson's criteria for poor prognosis:
    - At admit:
        * Age > 55
        * Leukocyte: >16,000
        * Glucose: >200
        * LDH: >350
        * AST: >250
    - At 48 hrs:
        * Arterial PO2: <60
        * HCO3: <20
        * Calcium: <8.0
        * BUN: Increase by 1.8+
        * Hematocrit: decrease by >10%
        * Fluid sequestration >6L
5. Treatment: IV fluids (best), analgesics, bowel rest
6. Complication: Pseudocyst

CHRONIC PANCREATITIS

1. Alcohol abuse
2. Triad: Pancreatic calcification (plain abdominal x-ray), steatorrhea (high fecal fat), and diabetes mellitus
3. Treatment: No alcohol, low fat diet

GASTROINTESTINAL

PANCREATIC CANCER

1. Most commonly located at pancreatic head
2. Presentation:
    - Jaundice and palpable non-tender gallbladder (Courvoisier's sign)
    - Troussoeau's sign- migratory phlebitis
3. Imaging: CT with contrast
4. Whipple procedure: remove antrum of stomach, part of duodenum, head of pancreas, gall bladder
5. Tumor Marker: CA 19-9

APPENDICITIS

1. Most common etiology: Fecalith
2. Umbilical pain, then pain over McBurney's point (RLQ)
3. Signs:
    - Rovsing – RLQ pain with palpation of LLQ
    - Obturator sign – RLQ pain with internal rotation of hip
    - Psoas sign - RLQ pn with hip flexion
4. Treatment: Appendectomy

CELIAC DISEASE

1. Small bowel inflammation from allergy to gluten
2. Diagnosis:
    - IgA anti endomysial and anti-tissue transglutaminase antibodies
    - Small bowel biopsy
3. Treatment: Lifelong gluten free diet

CROHN'S DISEASE

1. Characteristics:
    - Mouth to anus
    - Skip lesions
    - Transmural
    - Fistulas common
2. Barium enema: Cobblestone appearance
3. Treatment:
    - Flares: Prednisone +/- Mesalamine +/- Metronidazole or Ciprofloxacin
    - Maintenance: Mesalamine
    - Surgery is not curative. Adjacent portion of bowel is affected post-op

ULCERATIVE COLITIS

1. Characteristics:
    - Starts at rectum and moves proximal
    - Continuous lesions
    - Mucosal surface only

GASTROINTESTINAL SYSTEM

- → Risk of colon cancer
2. Barium enema: Lead pipe (loss of haustral markings)
3. Treatment:
   - → Colectomy is curative.
   - → Medications: Prednisone and mesalamine.

IRRITABLE BOWEL SYNDROME

1. Diagnosis of exclusion
2. Often associated with psychological pathology

INTUSSUSCEPTION

1. Presentation:
   - → Children after viral infections or adults with cancer
   - → Currant jelly stools. Sausage mass on palpation
2. Barium enema- Diagnostic and therapeutic in children

ISCHEMIC BOWEL

1. Most common artery: Superior mesenteric artery
2. Presentation:
   - → >50 years old with history of coronary artery disease
   - → Acute: Abdominal pain out of proportion to findings
   - → Chronic: pain 10-30 mins after eating, relieved by lying or squatting
3. Imaging:
   - → Plain films/CT: Bowel edema, pneumatosis intestinalis, portal venous gas
   - → Mesenteric angiography is the gold standard
3. Treatment:
   - → Supportive: Bowel rest, fluids, antibiotics
   - → Laparotomy with bowel resection for bowel infarction
   - → Revascularization is the gold standard

BOWEL ATRESIA

1. Signs and symptoms of bowel obstruction in first few days of life.

MECKEL'S DIVERTICULUM

1. Remnant of the omphalomesenteric duct
2. Rule of 2's: 2% of population, 2 feet proximal to ileocecal valve, 2" in length, 2 years of age
3. Presentation: Painless rectal bleed, obstructive signs or epigastric pain.

DIVERTICULITIS

1. Most common location: Sigmoid colon
2. Presentation: LLQ abdominal pain, fever and leukocytosis in older patients
3. CT: Fat stranding, bowel wall thickening
4. Treatment: Metronidazole and Ciprofloxacin. Bowel rest

GASTROINTESTINAL

TOXIC MEGACOLON

1. Complication of Ulcerative colitis (most common), Crohn's, Hirschsprung's, pseudomembranous colitis, enteritis
2. Presentation: Rigid abdomen
3. Plain film: Colonic distention
4. Treatment:
    → Decompression of colon, fluids, antibiotics
    → If no improvement in 24 hours, colectomy is indicated

HIRSCHSPRUNG'S DISEASE

1. Congenital megacolon
2. Presentation: Constipation and failure to thrive
3. Diagnosis:
    → Initial test: Barium enema
    → Definitive: Rectal biopsy- absence of ganglion cells
4. Treatment: Surgical correction

VOLVULUS

1. Bowel twists on itself
o   Most common: Sigmoid volvulus
2. Findings: Tympanic abdomen
3. Radiograph: "bent inner tube" or "coffee bean sign"
4. Treatment:
    → Emergent decompression (sigmoidoscopic or colonscopic placement of rectal tube for drainage)
    → Recurrence is common so elective colectomy is recommended post decompression

BOWEL OBSTRUCTION:

1. Etiology: Adhesion, hernia, fecal impact, volvulus, neoplasm
2. Presentation: Vomit partially digested food. Hyperactive then silent bowel sounds
3. Radiograph: Air fluid levels
4. Treatment: Bowel rest, NG tube placement, surgery as directed by underlying cause

HEREDITARY COLON CANCER SYNDROMES

1. Lynch Syndrome (HNPCC):
    → Most common.
    → Risk of adenocarcinoma- mean age 44.
    → Associated with ovarian and endometrial cancer
2. Familial Adenomatous polyposis:
    → 100-1,000s of adenoma polyps by age 30
    → Risk of adenocarcinoma and desmoid tumors
3. Peutz-Jegher's syndrome:
    → Hamartomatous polyps

GASTROINTESTINAL SYSTEM

COLON CANCER

1. Begin screening colonoscopy at age 50, every 10 years until age 85.
   - More likely to be malignant: sessile, >1 cm, villous
   - Less likely to be malignant: Pedunculated, <1 cm, tubular
2. Barium enema findings: Apple core appearance
3. Tumor Marker: CEA
4. Treatment: Resect tumors

ANAL FISSURE

1. Presentation: Tearing pain on defecation, bright red blood on toilet paper.
2. Treatment: Sitz baths

RECTAL ABSCESS

1. Location: most often perirectal/perianal
2. Treatment: Warm water cleanse, high fiber diet and surgical drainage

FECAL IMPACTION

1. Small amount of watery stool leakage
2. Proximal impaction:
   - May be neoplasm
   - Break up with colonoscopy/sigmoidoscopy
3. Distal impaction
   - Rock-hard stool on rectal exam
   - Treatment: Manually break up stool

HEMORRHOID

1. Varices of hemorrhoidal plexus
   - External- lower 1/3 of anus (below dentate line)
     * Associated with pain and pruritus
   - Internal- upper 1/3 of anus
     * Blood covered stool or toilet paper
2. Treatment: Fiber, sitz bath, reduction if needed

HERNIAS

1. Umbilical: congenital
2. Hiatal
   - Associated with GERD
   - May occur in newborn
     * Bowel sounds auscultated in chest.
     * Need to intubate, ventilate and suction through NG tube.
3. Inguinal hernia:
   - Indirect (most common)

GASTROINTESTINAL

- * Through internal inguinal ring into inguinal canal
- → Direct
  - * Through external inguinal ring/ Hesselbach's triangle

GASTROENTERITIS

1. Norovirus
   - → Associated with cruises
2. Rotavirus
   - → Associated with young children in winter
   - → Transmission: Person
   - → Vomiting and watery diarrhea.
   - → Supportive therapy
3. Staphylococcus toxin
   - → Transmission: Poultry, egg salad, picnic food
   - → Rapid onset vomiting.
   - → Supportive therapy
4. Bacillus cereus
   - → Toxin
   - → Transmission: Rice
   - → Watery diarrhea in less than 24 hours
5. Clostridium perfringens toxin
   - → Transmission: Raw meat and poultry
   - → Rapid onset, crampy diarrhea
6. Clostridium difficile
   - → Associated with recent antibiotic use
   - → Treatment: Flagyl or vancomycin PO
7. Vibrio vulnificus
   - → Transmission: Raw shellfish
8. Vibrio cholerae
   - → Transmission: Water
   - → Profuse watery diarrhea. "Rice water diarrhea"
   - → Supportive therapy
9. Giardia
   - → Transmission: water
   - → Nausea, bloating, diarrhea, foul smelling and greasy stool
     - * Symptoms develop weeks after exposure
   - → Treatment: Metronidazole
10. Cryptosporidia
    - → Immunosuppressed population
    - → Transmission: Water
    - → Vomiting, watery diarrhea
    - → Supportive therapy and HIV treatment

GASTROINTESTINAL

11. Cyclosporiasis
    - Immunocompromised, tropical countries
    - Transmission: Imported/uncooked foods
    - Watery diarrhea
    - Treatment: Sulfamethoxazole/trimethoprim
12. Listeria:
    - Transmission: unpasteurized cheese
13. Enterotoxic E. coli
    - Most common cause of Traveler's diarrhea
    - Transmission: Food
    - Watery diarrhea
    - Treatment: Bismuth and loperamide
14. Enterohemorrhagic E.coli
    - Invasive species
    - Transmission: Undercooked beef.
    - Purulent, bloody diarrhea, fever
    - Supportive therapy. Can cause hemolytic uremic syndrome.
15. Salmonella
    - Invasive species
    - S. enterica
        * Transmit: poultry
        * Purulent diarrhea, fever
        * Supportive therapy
    - S. typhi
        * Transmit: Fecal-oral
        * Typhoid fever, "pea soup diarrhea"
        * Treatment: Fluoroquinolones or Ceftriaxone and fluid replacement
    - Carriers- Cannot work in food industry. Should remove gallbladder
16. Shigella
    - Invasive species
    - Transmit: fecal-oral
    - Purulent bloody diarrhea, fever
    - Supportive therapy.
17. Campylobacter
    - Invasive species
    - Transmit: poultry
    - Purulent, bloody diarrhea, fever
    - Supportive therapy. Risk of Guillain-Barre

GASTROINTESTINAL

VITAMIN/NUTRITION DEFICIENCIES

Vitamin	At Risk Group	Deficiency
A	Elderly, alcoholics, liver disease	Night blindness, dry skin
C	Alcoholics, elderly men	Scurvy (poor wound healing, petechiae, bleeding gums)
D	Elderly, low sunlight	Rickets, Osteomalasia
E		Hemolytic anemia, degenerative nerve changes
K		Bleeding, elevated PT
Thiamine (B1)	Alcoholics, poverty	Beriberi (tingling, poor coordination, edema, cardiac dysfunction) Wernicke's encephalopathy (ataxia, confusion) Korsakoff syndrome (confabulation, retrograde and anterograde amnesia)
Niacin (B3)	Poverty, alcoholics	Pellegra (diarrhea, dermatitis, dementia)
Pantothenic Acid (B5)	Alcoholics	Numbness, tingling, headache, fatigue, insomina
Pyridoxine (B6)	Adolescents, alcoholics	Dermatitis, atrophic glossitis, sideroblastic anemia
Folate	Pregnancy, alcoholics	Neural tube defects, megaloblastic anemia, glossitis, confusion
Cobalamin (B12)	Elderly, vegans, atrophic gastritis	Megaloblastic anemia, subacute combined degeneration of spinal cord, seizures, dementia

PKU

1. Screening at birth
2. Can cause mental retardation
3. Treatment: Low phenylalanine diet and tyrosine supplementation by age 3

EAR EYE NOSE THROAT

BLEPHARITIS
1. Presentation: Seborrhea, greasy, scruf (dandruff), collarettes (scales)
2. Treatment: Lid scrubs

BLOWOUT FRACTURE
1. Presentation: Muscle entrapment, gaze restriction, double vision
2. Treatment: Prompt ophthalmic referral

CATARACT
1. Risk Factors: Aging, hypoparathyroid, steroid use, lovastatin use
2. Fundoscopy: "Black on red background."
3. Treatment: Surgical removal is definitive

CHALAZION
1. Sterile inflammation of zeis or meibomian gland
2. Presentation: Insidious, painless mass on lid
3. Treatment: Warm compresses

HORDEOLUM (STYE)
1. Most common organism: S. aureus
2. Presentation: Acute painful pustule on lid
3. Treatment: Warm compress

CONJUNCTIVITIS
1. Viral
   - Adenovirus (most common)
     * Presentation: Acute unilateral or bilateral erythema, watery eyes, and preauricular adenopathy
     * Associated with URI
     * Self limiting
   - HSV - Treatment: Acyclovir
2. Allergic
   - Bilateral, watery/stringy discharge
3. Bacterial
   - May be unilateral
   - Organisms:
     * S. pneumonia, S. aureus– Acute mucopurulent
     * M. catarrhalis, Gonococcal– non exudative, persistent
     * Chlamydia– newborn, purulent
   - Treatment: Antibiotic eye drops
     * Under 6 years old: Azithromycin
     * Adults: ciprofloxacin, tobramycin or gentamicin

EAR EYE NOSE THROAT

CORNEAL ABRASION

1. Severe pain, photophobia
2. Fluorescein staining
3. Treatment: Bacitracin-polymyxin ointment, acetaminophen
   → Patching: Only if abrasion >5mm. Never longer than 24 hours

CORNEAL ULCER

1. Presentation
   → Contact lenses
   → White spot on surface of cornea that stains with fluorescein
2. Treatment: Ciprofloxacin eye drops

DACRYOADENITIS

1. Lacrimal glad swelling
2. Presentation:
   * S shapedupper eyelid, may have lateral rectus involvement
   → Chronic
      * Most common
      * Painless
      * Associated with systemic disease
   → Acute:
      * Children/young adults
      * Etiology: Viral, S. aureus, Streptococcus spp.

DACRYOSTENOSIS

1. Lacrimal duct does not open in newborn
2. Treatment: Warm compress and massage. Self limiting

ECTROPION

1. Eyelid turned out

ENTROPION

1. Eyelid turned in

FOREIGN BODY

1. Fluorescein staining and woods lamp
2. Patching no longer than 24 hours
3. Gently remove, unless metallic or penetrating

GLAUCOMA

1. Primary open angle- most common.

EAR EYE NOSE THROAT

- → Aqueous outflow obstruction
- → Presentation
  - ✱ Often asymptomatic, >40 years of age, most common in African Americans
  - ✱ Peripheral field defect
- → Tonometry: >21
- → Treatment: Timolol, pilocarpine or acetazolamide

2. Acute angle closure
- → Iris against lens
- → Presentation:
  - ✱ Dark environment, acute loss of vision, nausea and vomiting
  - ✱ Steam corny, fixed and dilated pupil
- → Tonometry: >50
- → Treatment: Opthamology consult. Medication or surgery

HYPHEMA

1. Trauma causes blood in anterior chamber of eye
2. Treatment
   - → Elevate head at night, acetaminophen for pain, patch/shield
   - → Surgery if high pressure or persistent bleeding

MACULAR DEGENERATION

1. Presentation:
   - → Painless loss of central vision
   - → Elderly patients
   - → Metamorphopsia (distortion on Amsler grid)
2. Fundoscopy:
   - → Nonexudative: Drusden spot, macular atrophy
   - → Exudative: Hemorrhage, neovascularization

NYSTAGMUS

1. Down/upbeat- CNS dysfunction
2. Vestibular (horizontal)- labyrinth or vestibular nerve dysfunction
3. Gaze evoked- most common and often benign

OPTIC NEURITIS

1. Presentation:
   - → Acute monocular vision loss/blurriness and pain on extraocular movements
   - → Typically occurs over hours or days
2. Funduloscopy: Inflammation of the optic disc
3. Associated with multiple sclerosis

EAR EYE NOSE THROAT

ORBITAL CELLULITIS
1. Often associated with sinusitis
2. Occurs more often in children than adults
3. Treatment: Hospitalization and IV broad spectrum antibiotics

PAPILLEDEMA
1. Optic disc swelling due to increased ICP
   → Causes: Brain tumor/abscess, meningitis, cerebral hemorrhage, encephalitis, pseudotumor cerebri
2. Immediate neuroimaging to rule out mass lesion, then CSF analysis
3. Treatment: Underlying cause

VISION LOSS
1. First step: Check visual acuity
2. Lesion location:
   → One eye –before chiasm (optic nerve, retina, cornea, sclera or vasculature problem)
   → Bitemporal hemianopia –at optic chiasm
   → One visual field – after optic chiasm
     * Homonymous hemianopia –optic tract
     * Homonymous quadrantanopia – optic radiation
     * Homonymous hemianopia with central vision sparing –occipital lobe

PTERYGIUM
1. Only surgically remove when vision is affected

RETINAL DETACHMENT
1. Presentation: Vertical curtain coming down, may sense floaters or flashes at onset, loss of vision over several hours
2. Fundoscopy: See detachment
3. Treatment:
   → Consult ophthalmologist
   → Stay supine with head turned towards side of detached retina

AMAUROSIS FUGAX
1. Presentation: Transient monocular vision loss, vertical curtain coming down
2. Etiology: Embolism from carotid artery, ophthalmic artery and heart, or giant cell arteritis
3. Rule out carotid artery stenosis by carotid ultrasound

RETINAL VASCULAR OBSTRUCTION
1. Presentation: Sudden painless loss of vision
   → Branch vessel: Partial monocular vision loss
   → Central vessel: Complete monocular vision loss
2. Retinal artery obstruction:

EAR EYE NOSE THROAT

→ Fundoscopy:
  * Pale opaque fundus with red fovea and arterial attenuation
  * "Cherry red spot"
2. Retinal vein obstruction:
→ Fundoscopy:
  * Venous dilation and tortuosity, flame shaped retinal hemorrhages
  * "Blood and thunder retina"

RETINOPATHY
1. Leading cause of blindness
2. Etiology: Diabetes mellitus, hypertension, pre-eclampsia, eclampsia, blood dyscrasias, HIV
3. Proliferative type- Most severe. Neovascularizations seen on fundoscopy.

RETINOBLASTOMA
1. Presentation: Leukocoria in children

STRABISMUS
1. Presentation: Dysconjugate gaze in newborns
2. Treatment:
   → Patch exercises
   → If untreated after age 2, amblyopia results

OTITIS MEDIA
1. Population: Age 2 and under
2. Organisms: S. pneumoniae, H. influenzae, M. catarrhalis
3. Best test: Pneumatic Insufflation
4. Treatment: Amoxicillin is first line. For penicillin allergy, use erythromycin
5. Complications: Mastoiditis and bullous myringitis

BULLOUS MYRINGITIS
1. Physical exam: Bulging tympanic membrane
2. Etiology: Complication of acute otitis media or Mycoplasma infection
3. Treatment: Macrolide

RAMSAY HUNT SYNDROME
1. Etiology: Herpes Zoster
2. Presentation: Facial weakness, ipsilateral reduced lacrimation, vesicular lesions
3. Treatment: Acyclovir

HERPES SIMPLEX KERATITIS
1. Dendritic lesion on fluorescein stain

ACOUSTIC NEUROMA/VESTIBULAR SCHWANNOMA
1. Benign proliferation over CN VIII
2. Presentation: Unilateral sensorineural hearing loss, tinnitus, disequilibrium
3. Diagnostic study: MRI
4. Treatment: Surgery

EAR EYE NOSE THROAT

CHOLESTEATOMA

1. Presentation: Conductive hearing loss, unilateral, discharge (may be foul smelling), vertigo
2. Otoscope: White keratinized mass in tympanic membrane extends to middle ear and upper retraction
3. Treatment: Surgical removal

HEARING IMPAIRMENT

1. Rinne test:
   → Bone > Air in conductive hearing loss
   → Air >Bone in sensorineural hearing loss
2. Weber test:
   → Sound lateralizes to affected ear in conductive hearing loss
   → Sound lateralizes to unaffected ear in sensorineural hearing loss
3. Cerumen impaction, genetic disorders, infections, aging and excessive noise are the most common causes
4. Neurological deficits necessitate imaging

HEMATOMA OF EXTERNAL EAR

1. Presentation: Blunt trauma to ear
2. Treatment: Evacuate blood and cephalexin
   → Damage may result in cauliflower ear

MASTOIDITIS

1. Complication of acute otitis media.
2. Organisms: S. pneumoniae, H. influenzae, M. catarrhalis, S. aureus, S. pyogenes
3. Treatment: IV antibiotics (Ie. ceftriaxone)

LABYRINTHITIS

1. Presentation: Acute onset severe vertigo, hearing loss, tinnitus
2. Etiology: Usually viral
3. Treatment: Symptomatic (diazepam or meclizine vertigo, promethazine for nausea)
   → Self limiting in 1 to 2 weeks
   → Risk of meningitis

VESTIBULAR NEURITIS

1. Presentation: Acute onset vertigo without loss of hearing and tinnitus
2. Treatment: Symptomatic (diazepam or meclizine vertigo, promethazine for nausea)

MENIERE'S DISEASE:

1. Presentation:
   → Age 20-70
   → Vertigo attackslasting hours, fluctuating sensorineural hearing loss, tinnitus and aural pressure
2. Treatment:

EAR EYE NOSE THROAT

- → Maintenance: Diuretic and sodium restriction.
- → Acute attacks: Meclizine, diazepam, promethazine

BENIGN PAROXYSMAL POSITIONAL VERTIGO

1. Etiology:
   - → Young- trauma
   - → Elderly- generative processes
2. Presentation: Vertigo spells lasting a minute or two associated with positional change or visual change
3. Physical Exam: Dix-Hallpike (AKA Nylen-Barany) maneuver reproduces symptoms (quick head turn when patient is supine)
4. Treatment: Epley or Semont maneuver

OTITIS EXTERNA

1. Etiology: Pseudomonas aeruginosa (swimmer's ear), S. aureus (digital trauma)
2. Physical exam: Pain movement of pinna
3. Treatment: Ciprofloxacin ear drops

TYMPANIC PERFORATION

1. Treatment:
   - → Most heal spontaneously, keep clean and dry
   - → Surgery if persists past 2 months

BAROTRAUMA

1. Presentation: Ear pain associated with pressure changes (Ie. diving, flying)
2. Treatment: Autoinflation and decongestants

SINUSITIS

1. Presentation:
   - → After URI
   - → Headache, pain leaning forward. Facial tap elicits pain.
2. Viral:
   - → Most common
   - → Symptoms < 7 days
3. Bacterial:
   - → Symptoms 7+ days and associated with bilateral purulent nasal discharge
   - → Organisms: S. pneumoniae, H. influenzae, M. catarhalis
   - → Treatment: Amoxicilin
4. Chronic:
   - → Imaging- CT (best test) or Waters' view radiograph

COMMON COLD (RHINOPHARYNGITIS)

1. Etiology: Rhinovirus
   - → Air droplet transmission

EAR EYE NOSE THROAT

1. Treatment: Only symptomatic treatment until after 1 week
   → Time is the most important factor in treatment decision-making

ALLERGIC RHINITIS

1. Presentation: Clear nasal drainage, pruritis, pale, bluish, boggy mucosa
2. Treatment: Intranasal corticosteroids is best

VASOMOTOR RHINITIS

1. Presentation: Precipitated by change in temp, humidity, odors, alcohol

EPISTAXIS

1. Etiology:
   → Digital trauma or URI in children
   → Hypertension or coagulopathy in adults
2. Presentation: Generally unilateral nose bleed <30 minutes
3. Treatment:
   → Child: Lean forward, pinch nose
      * If resistant, pack it
      * If still resistant, ablation
   → Adult: Control hypertension or coagulopathy
4. Kesselbach's plexus- anterior bleed
5. Woodruff's plexus- posterior bleed
   → Emergent evaluation

NASAL TRAUMA

1. Perform CT to rule out septal hematoma. If present, refer to ENT surgery to prevent saddle nose deformity

FOREIGN BODY (EAR)

1. Child- Pain, purulence
   → Treatment: Removal, antibiotics
2. Homeless- Buzzing in ear
   → Treatment: No light in ear. Lidocaine drop in ear to paralyze bug, then remove.

NASAL POLYP

1. Usually benign
2. Disease association:
   → Most often: Allergic rhinitis
   → Consider Cystic Fibrosis when multiple polyps are seen

ACUTE PHARYNGITIS

1. Viral
   → Adenovirus
   → Most common

EAR EYE NOSE THROAT

→ Treatment: Symptomatic. Wait 10 days before giving antibiotics
1. Group A Streptococcal pharyngitis
   → Organism: S. pyogenes
   → Centor Criteria:
       * Absence of cough
       * Exudates
       * Fever
       * Cervical lymphadenopathy
   → Rapid strep test and throat culture
   → Treatment: Amoxicillin
   → Complications: Rheumatic fever and post-strep glomerulonephritis

INFECTIOUS MONONUCLEOSIS
1. Etiology: Epstein Barr virus
2. Presentation: Fever, sore throat, lymphadenopathy, splenomegaly
3. Diagnostic studies:
   → Atypical lymphocytosis
   → Positive monospot test
4. Treatment: Symptomatic and avoid contact sports
   → Ampicillin and amoxicillin cause rash

HAND-FOOT MOUTH
1. Etiology: Coxsackievirus A
2. Presentations: Non-tender vesicles on hand, foot mouth
3. Treatment: Self limiting

APHTHOUS ULCERS (CANKER SORE)
1. Etiology: Idiopathic
2. Presentation: Recurrent erosions – yellow, red halos
3. Treatment: Symptomatic (viscous lidocaine)

ORAL CANDIDIASIS
1. Presentation:
   → Immunocompromised, young patients
   → Painful, white fluffy patches that can be scraped off, leaving an erythematous, friable base
2. Treatment: Nystatin mouth wash

ORAL HERPES SIMPLEX
1. Etiology: HSV type 1
2. Presentation: Vesicular lesions all in the same stage of development

ORAL LEUKOPLAKIA
1. Presentation:

EAR EYE NOSE THROAT

- Smokers, AIDs, alcohol abuse
- Painless, precancerous white lesions that cannot be scraped off

ORAL LICHEN PLANUS

1. Etiology: Chronic inflammation, autoimmune
2. Presentation: Lacy leukoplakia

ORAL CANCER

1. Most often squamous cell carcinoma

ORAL HAIRY LEUKOPLAKIA

1. Etiology: Epstein-barr virus.
2. Presentation:
   - Immunocrompromised patients
   - Whitish-tan with feathery appearance on lateral border of tongue

EPIGLOTTITIS

1. Organisms: H. influenza type B, Strep spp., Staph spp.
2. Presentation: Unvaccinated patient leaning forward, drooling, stridor
3. Physical exam: Never visualize
4. Lateral radiograph: Thumbprint sign
5. Treatment: Secure airway, IV Ceftriaxone and IV fluids

LARYNGITIS

1. Etiology: Viral
2. Presentation: Hoarseness following a URI
3. Treatment: Relax voice, supportive

PERITONSILLAR ABSCESS

1. Presentation: Hot potato voice, deviated uvula and soft palate
2. Treatment:
   - Surgical drainage
   - Clindamycin or metronidazole + penicillin G
   - "Quinsy" Tonsillectomy may be indicated

PAROTITIS

1. Etiology: Parainfluenza virus. Mump virus prior to vaccination.

SIALADENITIS

1. Infected salivary gland
2. Etiology: S. aureus
   - Usually due to obstruction or gland hyposecretion
3. Treatment:
   - Antibiotics: Dicloxacillin, 1st gen cephalosporin, or clindamycin
   - Symptomatic: Hydration, sialalogues

PULMONARY

ACUTE BRONCHITIS

1. Organisms:
   → Most common: Viral
   → Chronic lung patients: H. influenzae, S. pneumoniae, M. catarrhalis
2. Presentation:
   → Cough, fever, constitutional symptoms
   → Typically less severe than pneumonia, normal vital signs, no rales, no egophony
3. Chest radiograph: Normal
4. Treatment:
   → Most patients-Symptomatic treatment
   → Exacerbation of chronic bronchitis- second generation cephalosporin

PNEUMONIA

1. Presentation: Tachycardia, tachypnea, dyspnea, febrile, age 65+
2. Physical exam: Egophony, fremitus, rales
3. Chest radiograph: Infiltrates and or consolidation
4. Treatment:
   → Community Acquired:
     * Adult:
       - Healthy patients:
         ▸ First line: Macrolide *(Azithro, Clarithro, Erythro)*
         ▸ Second line: Doxycycline
       - Comorbidities:
         ▸ First line: Fluoroquinolon
         ▸ Second line: Beta-lactam + Macrolide *(Unasyn/Zosyn/Augmentin)*
     * Child:
       - First line: Amoxicillin
       - Second line: 2nd or 3rd generation Cephalosporin, Clindamycin or Macrolide
   → Hospital Acquired (HAC): Vancomycin + Piperacillin/Tazobactam *(Zosyn)*
   → AIDs patients receive Bactrim prophylaxis against PCP pneumonia
     * Dapsone is second line
   → Admission criteria: CURB-65
     * Confusion, Urea >7, RR >30, BP <90/<60, age >65
     * 3+ points requires admission

Pathogen	Who	Presentation
Streptococcus pneumoniae	MOST COMMON, Post-splenectomy	Rust colored sputum, single rigor. Lobar infiltrate
Mycoplasma pneumoniae	College student	Walking pneumonia: low temp, bullous myringitis
Klebsiella pneumoniae	Alcohol abuse, chronic illness	Currant jelly sputum

PULMONARY:

Legionella pneumophia	Air conditioning, aerosolized water	
Chlamydia pneumoniae	College kids	Long prodrome, sore throat
Pseudomonas spp.	Cystic fibrosis *HAC: Ventilator associated	
Haemophilus influenzae	COPD, smokers Post-splenectomy	
Pneumocystis jiroveci	HIV CD4 <200, immunosuppressed	Slow onset, increased LDH, interstitial infiltrates, bilateral
Staphylococcus spp.	After influenza/viral infection *HAC (MRSA)	
Fungus	Leukemia, lymphoma, immunosuppressed, AIDs	
RSV	Children <1 year old	
Parainfluenza	Children 2-5 years old	

ACUTE BRONCHIOLITIS
1. Most often cause by RSV
2. Presentation:
   → Infants, young children
   → Tachypnea, respiratory distress, wheezing
3. Treatment:
   → RSV- admit, IV ribavirin
   → Not RSV- supportive, suction

CROUP (LARYNGOTRACHEOBRONCHITIS)
1. Etiology: Parainfluenza virus
2. Presentation:
   → Winter, patients < 3 years old
   → Barking cough, stridor at night
3. AP radiograph: "Steeple sign"
4. Treatment:
   → Supportive (air humidifier)
   → Severe: IV fluids and racemic epinepherine

INFLUENZA
1. Presentation: Fevers, chills, coryza, myalgia
2. Treatment:
   → Oseltamivir or zanamivir before 48 hours
   → Supportive therapy
3. Annual vaccine recommended for all, unless contraindicated

PULMONARY

PERTUSSIS (WHOOPING COUGH)

1. Organism: Bordetella pertussis (gram negative capsule)
2. Presentation:
   → Patients < 2 years old
   → Catarrhal stage: Cold-like symptoms, poor feeding and sleeping
   → Paroxysmal stage: high-pitched whooping cough
   → Convalescent stage: residual cough (100 days)
3. Diagnostic studies: Lymphocytosis
4. Treatment: Macrolide *Azithro, Erythro, Clarithro*
5. Vaccine: Tdap, DTaP

TUBERCULOSIS

1. Organism: Mycobacterium tuberculosis
2. Presentation: Cough, night sweats, weight loss, post-tussive rales, endemic area, immunocompromised.
3. Xray: cavitary lesions, infiltrates, gohn complexes in apex of lungs
4. Acid-fast bacilli stain
5. Biopsy: Caseating granulomas
6. Mantoux TST: Test is positive if induration (PPD)
   → >5 mm in immunosuppressed patients
   → >10 in patients age <4 or has risk factors
   → >15mm if there are no risk factors
7. Treatment:
   → Latent treatment: Isoniazid for 9 months
   → Active quad therapy: Isoniazid, Rifampin, Ethambutol, Pyrazinamide for 8 weeks *RIPE*
      * Isoniazid- peripheral neuropathy (give with B6)
      * Rifampin- orange body fluids, hepatitis
      * Ethambutol- Optic neuritis, red-green blindness
      * Pyrazinamide- hyperuricemia
8. Prophylaxis for household members: Isoniazid for 1 year

CARCINOID TUMORS

1. Most common type: Adenoma
2. Slow growing, rare metastasis
3. Presentation:
   → Carcinoid syndrome- Flushing, diarrhea, telangiectasis
4. Diagnostics studies:
   → Bronchoscopy- pink/purple central lesion, well vascularized. Pedunculated or sessile
   → Elevated 5-HIAA
5. Treatment: Surgical removal

LUNG CANCER

1. Small cell

PULMONARY

- Location: Central, very aggressive
- Treatment: Combination chemotherapy needed
- Paraneoplastic syndromes: Cushings, SIADH

1. Non-small cell:
   - Squamous cell
     * Location: central
     * May cause hemoptysis
     * Paraneoplastic syndrome: hypercalcemia
       - Elevated PTH-rp
   - Large Cell
     * Location: Periphery 60%
     * Paraneoplastic syndrome: Gynecomastia
   - Adenocarcinoma
     * Most common
     * Associated with smoking and asbestos exposure
     * Location: Periphery
     * Paraneoplastic syndrome: Thrombophlebitis
   - Treatment: Resection
2. Associated manifestations:
   - Superior vena cava syndrome (facial/arm edema and swollen chest wall veins)
   - Pancoast tumor (shoulder pain, Horner's syndrome, brachial plexus compression)
   - Horner's syndrome (unilateral miosis, ptosis and anhidrosis)
   - Carcinoid syndrome (flushing, diarrhea and telangiectasis)

PULMONARY NODULE

1. Stable if <2 cm or not changing

ASTHMA

1. Presentation: Most often young patients present with wheezing and dyspnea often associated with illness, exercise and allergic triggers
2. Diagnosis: Greater than 12% increase in FEV1 after bronchodilator therapy.
3. Treatment guidelines:
   - Intermittent: Less than 2 times per week or 3 night symptoms per month
     * Step 1: Short acting beta2 agonist (SABA) PRN
   - Mild Persistent: More than 2 times per week or 3-4 night symptoms per month
     * Step 2: Low-Dose inhaled corticosteroids (ICS) daily
   - Moderate Persistent: Daily symptoms or more than 1 nightly episode per week
     * Step 3: Low-Dose ICS + Long acting beta2 agonist (LABA) daily
     * Step 4: Medium-Dose ICS +LABA daily
   - Severe Persistent: Symptoms several times per day and nightly
     * Step 5: High-Dose ICS +LABA daily
     * Step 6: High-Dose ICS +LABA +oral steroids daily
   - Acute treatment:
     * Oxygen, nebulized SABA, ipratropium bromide and oral corticosteroids

PULMONARY

BRONCHIECTASIS

1. Dilated airways.
2. Etiology: ½ of cases are due to CF
3. Presentation: Copious foul smelling sputum, frequent respiratory infections, chronic cough
4. Radiograph: Dilated, thickened airways and scattered opacities. "Tram-tracks"
5. Treatment: Chest physiotherapy and antibiotics for acute exacerbations

CYSTIC FIBROSIS

1. Etiology: Autosomal recessive mutation in CFTR gene
   → Abnormally thick mucus, difficulty clearing mucus
2. Presentation: Recurrent respiratory infections (especially Pseudomonas), steatorrhea
3. Diagnosis: Quantitative sweat chloride test
4. Treatment:
   → Maintenance: Chest physiotherapy, high fat diet, supplement fat soluble vitamins (A, D, E, K)
   → Acute exacerbations: Antibiotics

CHRONIC OBSTRUCTIVE PULMONARY DISEASE

1. Chronic bronchitis:
   → Presentation: "Blue bloaters"
   → Physical exam: Rales, ronchi
   → Chest radiograph: peribronchial and perivascular markings
2. Emphysema:
   → Presentation: "Pink puffers"
   → Physical Exam: Decreased lung sounds
   → Chest radiograph: parenchymal bullae (subpleural blebs) are pathognomonic
3. Treatment:
   → Smoking cessation, supplemental O2.
   → Medications: Short acting bronchodilators for mild disease, long acting bronchodilators +/- inhaled corticosteroids for moderate to severe disease
   → Antibiotics for acute exacerbations

PLEURAL EFFUSION

1. Differentiate exudate and transudate with pleurocentesis and Light's Criteria
2. *Exudate*: Increased protein or LDH. Infection, malignancy, trauma
3. *Transudate*: Congestive heart failure, atelectasis, cirrhosis
4. Chest radiograph: Blunting of costophrenic angle. Mediastinum shift away from effusion.

PNEUMOTHORAX

1. Spontaneous:
   → Population: Tall thin males 10-30 years old
   → Treatment: If > 15%, chest tube insertion with serial radiographs
2. Tension:
   → Etiology: Penetrating injury
   → Physical exam: Hyperresonance to percussion and trachea shift to contralateral side.

PULMONARY

→ Treatment: Large bore needle decompression 2nd intercostals space mid clavicular line.
1. Chest Radiograph: Visceral pleural line and deep sulcus sign

HEMOTHORAX
1. Etiology: Stab wound
2. Physical exam: Dullness to percussion, decreased breath sounds

ATELECTASIS
1. Presentation
   → Post-operative patients
   → Trachea shifted towards affected lung
2. Prevention: Incentive spirometry
3. Treatment: Physiotherapy, oxygen and continuous positive airway pressure

COR PULMONALE
1. Right ventricular enlargement and subsequent heart failure due to lung problem causing pulmonary artery hypertension
2. Etiology: COPD (most common), pulmonary embolism, acute respiratory distress syndrome
3. Physical Exam: Lower extremity edema, neck vein distention, hepatomegaly, parasternal lift, tricuspid/pulmonic insufficiency, loud S2
4. EKG: S1Q3T3

PULMONARY EMBOLISM
1. Presentation:
   → Vichow's triad: hypercoagulable state, venous stasis, vascular injury
   → Risk factors: Cancer, surgery, oral contraceptive pills, pregnancy, long bone fracture (fat emboli)
   → Homan's sign: (Dorsiflexion of foot causes pain in calf) indicative of deep vein thrombosis
2. EKG: Tachycardia (most common), ST changes, S1Q3T3 (Indicates cor pulmonale)
3. Imaging:
   → Spiral CT: Best initial test
   → Angiogram is gold standard
   → Chest radiograph: "Hampton's hump" (wedge shaped infarct)
4. Treatment: Heparin to Coumadin bridge. 3-6 mo treatment

PULMONARY HYPERTENSION
1. Pulmonary artery pressure >25 mmHg
   → May cause right ventricular hypertrophy
2. Presentation: Dyspnea on exertion, fatigue, chest pain, edema
3. Physical Exam: Loud P2, systolic ejection click, parasternal lift

IDIOPATHIC PULMONARY FIBROSIS
1. Physical exam: Inspiratory crackles
2. CT: Diffuse, patchy fibrosis with pleural honey-combing, reticular opacities
3. FEV1/FVC ratio: Increased

PULMONARY

COAL WORKER'S PNEUMOCONIOSIS

1. Population: Coal miners
2. Chest radiograph: Nodular opacities

ASBESTOSIS

1. Population: Workers in insulation, demolition, construction
2. Biopsy: Asbestos bodies
3. Chest radiograph: Pleural and base lesions
4. Risk of mesothelioma

SILICOSIS

1. Population: Workers in mining, sand blasting, quarry work, stone work
2. Chest radiograph: Nodular opacities upper lungs

BERRYLIOSIS

1. Population: Workers in high-technology fields
2. Chest radiograph: Diffuse infiltrates, hilar lymphadenopathy
3. Treatment: Requires chronic steroids

SARCOIDOSIS

1. Presentation: Pulmonary manifestations (most common), erythema nodosum, parotid gland enlargement
2. Chest radiograph: Bilateral hilar lymphadenopathy. Reticular infiltrates.
3. Biopsy: non-caseating granulomas
4. Treatment: Steroids

ACUTE RESPIRATORY DISTRESS SYNDROME

1. Non-cardiogenic pulmonary edema
2. Etiology: Sepsis, severe trauma, aspiration of gastric contents, near drowning
3. Presentation: Tachypnea, pink frothy sputum, crackles
4. Diagnostic studies:
   - Chest radiograph: Bilaterally fluffy infiltrate
   - Normal BNP, pulmonary wedge pressure, left ventricle function and echocardiogram
5. Treatment: Underlying cause and intubation positive pressure oxygen

HYALIN MEMBRANE DISEASE

1. Etiology: Insufficient surfactant
2. Population: Pre-term newborn
3. Chest radiograph: Ground glass appearance, air bronchograms, bilateral atelectasis

PULMONARY

1. Treatment: Ventilation and steroids

FOREIGN BODY ASPIRATION

1. Complications: Pneumonia, acute respiratory distress syndrome, asphyxia
2. Treatment: Remove foreign body with bronchoscope

CARDIOVASCULAR SYSTEM

DILATED CARDIOMYOPATHY

1. Reduced contraction strength, large heart
2. Most common cardiomyopathy
3. Etiology: Genetics, excess alcohol, post-partum, chemotherapy, endocrine disorders
4. Physical exam: Dyspnea, S3 gallop, rales, jugular venous distention
5. Treatment:
   → Abstain from alcohol
   → Medications: ACE inhibitors, diuretics

TAKOTSUBO

1. Dilated cardiomyopathy, clinically indistinguishable from acute MI of anterior wall
2. "Heart break heart"- major catecholamine release
3. Imaging studies: Base of left ventricle is hyperkinetic, remainder of heart is akinetic
4. Treatment: Supportive. Disease is self limiting

HYPERTROPHIC CARDIOMYOPATHY

1. Hypertrophic portion of septum
2. Presentation: Young athlete with a positive family history has sudden death or syncopal episode.
3. Physical Exam:
   → Sustained PMI, bifid pulse, S4 gallop
   → Murmur: High pitched mid systolic murmur at LLSB. Increased with valsalva and standing (less blood in chamber). Decreased with squatting (more blood in chamber)
3. Treatment:
   → Refrain from vigorous physical activity
   → Medical: Beta blockers or calcium channel blockers
   → Surgical: Surgical or alcohol ablation of hypertrophied septum and defibrillator insertion

RESTRICTIVE CARDIOMYOPATHY

1. Etiology: Amyloidosis, sarcoidosis
2. Treatment: Nonspecific. Diuretics, ACE inhibitors, Calcium channel blockers

ATRIAL FIBRILLATION

1. Presentation:
   → Elderly, excessive alcohol use
   → Symptoms range from syncope, dyspnea, palpitations to no symptoms
   → Irregularly irregular pulse
2. EKG: Heart rate is irregularly irregular. Absense of P waves. Narrow QRS complex
3. Treatment:
   → Rate: Calcium channel blocker (diltiazem, verapamil) or beta blocker (metoprolol)
   → Rhythm:
      * Duration <48 hours- cardioversion, amiodarone (obtain echo to determine if clot is present prior to cardioversion)
      * Duration >48 hours- anticoagulate for 21 days prior to cardioversion

CARDIOVASCULAR SYSTEM

- Anticoagulation:
  * Determine need for anticoagulation by using CHADS2 to assess risk of stroke
    - Congestive heart failure –1 point
    - Hypertension –1 point
    - Age > 75–1 point
    - Diabetes Mellitus – 1 point
    - Stroke history – 2 points
  * 2 or more points – Heparin to Coumadin bridge
    - INR goal: 2 - 3
  * 1 point – Aspirin or Coumadin
  * 0 points – No therapy or Aspirin

ATRIAL FLUTTER
1. EKG: Regular, sawtooth pattern, atrial rate 250-350 BPM, narrow QRS complex
2. Occasionally occurs in COPD, congestive heart failure, atrial septal defect, coronary artery disease
3. Similar treatment as atrial fibrillation.

ATRIOVENTRICULAR BLOCK
1. 1st degree: PR interval > .2 seconds
2. 2nd degree type 1- longer, longer, drop- Wenckebach
3. 2nd degree type 2- some beats don't get through- Mobitz type 2
4. 3rd degree: P's and Q's don't agree. Block is 3rd degree.

BUNDLE BRANCH BLOCK
1. QRS complex > .12 seconds
2. May be due to MI
3. Left: R and R' (upward bunny ears) in V4-V6
4. Right: R and R' (upward bunny ears) in V1-V3

SUPERVENTRICULAR TACHYCARDIA
1. Heart rate: 150-250 BPM
2. Types:
   - Paroxysmal SVT - no structural abnormalities
   - AV nodal reentrant tachycardia
   - Wolf Parkinson White - Bundle of Kent fibers and delta wave on EKG
3. Treatment:
   - Valsalva for stable patients
   - Adenosine for symptomatic patients.
   - Definitive treatment: Radiofrequency ablation
   - WPW- do not administer adenosine nor calcium channel blockers

PREMATURE BEATS
1. Premature atrial(PAC) and ventricular (PVC) contractions
2. Presentation:
   - Typically benign. May cause palpitations.
   - Increased frequency with stimulants (Ie. Caffeine)

CARDIOVASCULAR SYSTEM

3. EKG: Irregular beats
   - PVC- widened QRS
   - PAC- abnormally shaped P wave
   - Every 3rd beat- trigeminy. Every other beat- bigeminy.
4. Treatment: None or beta blockers if symptomatic

SICK SINUS SYNDROME:
1. Population: Elderly
2. Periods of bradycardia and/or tachycardia
3. Treatment: Pacemaker

MULTIFOCAL ATRIAL TACHYCARDIA
1. EKG: Irregular tachycardia, narrow QRS complex, abnormally shaped P waves with different morphology

VENTRICULAR TACHYCARDIA
1. EKG: Wide complex tachycardia
2. Treatment:
   - Stable- amiodarone, lidocaine
   - Unstable- CPR and defibrillation

LONG QT SYNDROME
1. Etiology: Congenital or acquired (hypokalemia, medications: antiarrythmics, antifungal, antimalarials, 2. 2.
2. EKG: QT interval >0.45 seconds
3. Risk of syncope and sudden death
4. Treatment: Treat underlying cause, beta blockers for congenital disease. Implantable defibrillator

BRUGADA SYNDROME
1. Population: Asian men
2. Presentation: Syncope, ventricular fibrillation and sudden death
3. EKG: J point elevation in leads V1-V3 all the time or after antiarrhythmic medication administration
4. Treatment: Implantable defibrillator

VENTRICULAR FIBRILLATION
1. Presentation: Unstable patient.
2. EKG: No discernible heart contractions.
3. Treatment: CPR and defibrillation (AKA non-synchronized cardioversion)

TORSADES DE POINTES
1. EKG: Polymorphic ventricular tachycardia that appears to be twisting around a baseline
2. Etiology: Hypokalemia or hypomagnesemia
3. Treatment: IV Magnesium sulfate

CARDIOVASCULAR SYSTEM

BRADYCARDIA

1. Heart rate: < 60 BPM
2. Treatment: Atropine

ATRIAL SEPTAL DEFECT

1. Noncyanotic. Foramen ovale fails to close. Ostium secondum is most common.
2. Physical Exam: Wide fix split S2. Systolic murmur second left intercostals space. Failure to thrive.
3. Diagnosis: Best diagnosed by passing catheter through defect.
4. Treatment:
   → Symptomatic: Diuretics, ACE inhibitors, digoxin
   → Definitive: Surgical closure

COARCTATION OF THE AORTA

1. Noncyanotic.
2. Population: Turner's syndrome
3. Physical exam: Bounding pulses and elevated BP in upper extremities. Weak pulses in lower extremities
4. Chest radiograph: "Figure of 3 sign" *rib notching*

PATENT DUCTUS ARTERIOSUS

1. Noncyanotic.
2. Population: Preterm infants
3. Physical exam:
   → Wide pulse pressures. Bounding pulses.
   → Continuous machine like murmur at second intercostals space
4. Treatment: Indomethacin if preterm

VENTRICULAR SEPTAL DEFECT

1. Noncyanotic.
2. Presentation: Variable- asymptomatic to symptoms of heart failure
3. Physical exam: Pansystolic murmur at left sternal border.
4. Treatment: Most close by age 6, surgery if large

TETRALOGY OF FALLOT

1. Pulmonary stenosis, Right ventricular hypertrophy, overriding aorta, ventricular septal defect.
2. Presentation: Difficult feeding, failure to thrive. Tet spells (episodes of cyanosis).
3. Physical exam: Systolic ejection murmur radiating to the back.
4. Chest radiograph: Boot shaped heart

HEART FAILURE

1. Presentation/Examination:
   → Right sided: Jugular venous distention, edema, hepatomegaly

CARDIOVASCULAR SYSTEM

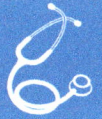

- → Left sided: Paroxysmal nocturnal dyspnea, S3 gallop, cough, orthopnea, rales
2. Chest radiograph: Kerley B lines.
3. BNP: elevated
4. Treatment: *Lasix (loop)*
   - → Acute – IV furosemide, upright posture, nitroglycerin
   - → Chronic (EF < 40%) – diuretic, ACE inhibitors, beta blocker *CHF*

METABOLIC SYNDROME

1. Triglycerides: > 150
2. HDL < 40 for males, < 50 for females
3. Blood pressure: >130/>85
4. Fasting plasma glucose: > 100 mg/dL
5. Waist circumference: 40+" for males, 35+" for females

ESSENTIAL HYPERTENSION

1. Stage 1: 140-159/90-99 x 2 readings
2. Stage 2: 160-179/100-109 x 2 readings
3. Resistant: not controlled after 3 medications. Refractory: not controlled after 5 meds.
4. Patients under 50- diastolic pressure better indicator of heart disease. Over 50- systolic pressure.
5. Treatment:
   - → Diuretics: *Thiazides (HCTZ)*
     - ✱ Distal tubule: Hydrochlorothiazide, chlorthiadone, Indapamide
       - • Side effect: Hypokalemia
     - ✱ Loop: Furosemide / *Lasix*
       - • Only CHF or renal failure
     - ✱ Potassium sparing- Spironalactone
       - • Side effect: Gynecomastia, hyperkalemia
     - ✱ Typically first choice
   - → ACE inhibitors:
     - ✱ Lisinopril
     - ✱ Side effects: Hyperkalemia. Cough or angioedema (Switch to ARB)
     - ✱ Not effective in African Americans. First in patients with CKD and DM.
   - → ARBs ('sartans):
     - ✱ Losartan, Valsartan, Irbersartan, Olmesartan
   - → Calcium Channel blockers:
     - ✱ Dihyropirimines: Amlodipine, nifedipine
     - ✱ Nondihyropirimines: Not used for blood pressure, used for heart
     - ✱ Side Effects: peripheral edema, CHF exacerbation, flushing
   - → Beta blockers:
     - ✱ Metoprolol, carvedilol (also alpha blocker). Labetalol (also alpha blocker)
     - ✱ Side Effects: decreased HR, bronchospasm
   - → Central acting: Clonidine
   - → Vasodilators: Hydralazine

CARDIOVASCULAR SYSTEM

- Safe in pregnancy: Methyl dopa, hydralazine, labetalol, nifedipine
- Goal: 140/90 for most patients. Diabetes or CKD- 130/80

SECONDARY HYPERTENSION

1. Sleep apnea, pheochromacytoma, coarctation of the aorta, parenchymal renal disease, renal artery stenosis, Cushing syndrome, primary hyperaldosteronism (Conn's disease)
2. Treat underlying cause

HYPERTENSIVE EMERGENCY

1. Presentation: BP usually >180/120 with impeding or progressing end organ damage
- Encephalopathy, stroke, papilledema, pulmonary edema, aortic dissection, renal failure, eclampsia

2. Treatment: IV labetalol or calcium channel blocker (dihydripyridine)

HYPERTENSIVE URGENCY

1. High blood pressure: usually 180/120 without signs of end organ damage
2. Treatment: oral antihypertensive

CARDIOGENIC SHOCK

1. Common causes: acute MI, heart failure, cardiac tamponade
2. Physical exam: Hypotension (SBP <90mmg), cyanosis, cool extremities, altered mental status, crackles
3. Treatment: Fluid resuscitation, pressors (dopamine), and treat underlying cause

ORTHOSTATIC HYPOTENSION

1. 20mmHg drop in systolic BP, 10 mmHg drop in diastolic pressure, 15 BPM increase in pulse when patient moves from supine/sitting to standing.

ACUTE MYOCARDIAL INFARCTION

1. Location of heart:
- Lateral (I, aVL, V5, V6): Left circumflex
- Anterior (V2-V4): Left anterior descending
- Septal (V1, V2): Left anterior descending
- Anterolateral (V4, V5, V6): Left main
- Posterior (V1, V2: ST depression): Right coronary artery
- Inferior (II, III, aVF): Right coronary artery

2. Serial cardiac enzymes:
- Troponins I and T:
  - Troponin I – most specific test
  - Elevate in 3-12 hours
- Myoglobin: Elevate in 1- 4 hours
- CK-MB: Elevate in 3-12 hours

PANCE/PANRE Study Guide

CARDIOVASCULAR SYSTEM

3. EKG:
   → ST elevation: acute ischemia
   → T wave depression: myocardial injury *ischemia*
   → Q wave: Infarct
4. Treatment:
   → 1st: Aspirin
   → Nitroglycerin, Morphine, Beta blocker, Oxygen
   → Percutaneous coronary intervention within 90 minutes or tPA within 3 hours
   → Patient should also go home on ACE inhibtors
   → Cocaine induced MI:
       * No beta blockers
       * Treat with calcium channel blocker (verapamil)

DRESSLER'S SYNDROME

1. Myocardial infarction complication, occurs 1-2 weeks post-MI
2. Presentation: Pericarditis, fever, leukocytosis
3. Treatment: Aspirin

ANGINA PECTORIS

1. Chest pain from myocardial ischemia
   → Stable- Relieved by rest.
   → Unstable- Occurring at rest.
   → Prinzmentals- vasospasm. Preservation of exercise capacity
2. Stress test: Reversible wall motion abnormalities/ ST depression >1 mm
3. Angiography- definitive diagnosis
4. Treatment:
   → Beta blockers, nitroglycerin.
   → Severe: angioplasty and bypass.

AORTIC ANEURYSM

1. Presentation: Flank pain, hypotension, pulsatile abdominal mass
2. Screening: Ultrasound, if male >65 and ever a smoker
3. Treatment:
   → Surgical repair if >5.5 cm or expands >0.6 cm per year
   → Monitor annually if >3 cm. Monitor every 6 months if >4 cm
   → Beta blocker

AORTIC DISSECTION

1. Sudden onset tearing chest pain, between scapulas. Diminished pulses
2. Chest radiograph: Widened mediastinum
3. Treatment:
   → Ascending aorta- Surgical emergency
   → Descending aorta- Medical therapy (beta blockers) unless complications are present

CARDIOVASCULAR SYSTEM

GIANT CELL ARTERITIS

1. Inflammation of large and medium vessels.
   → Temporal arteritis: most common manifestation
2. Presentation: Headache, scalp pain, jaw pain, visual changes and nodular, tender temporal artery
   → Associated with polymyalgia rheumatica
3. Definitive diagnosis: Temporal artery biopsy
4. Treatment: High dose prednisone – do urgently to prevent blindness (Do not wait for biopsy results)

PERIPHERAL ARTERY DISEASE

1. Presentation:
   → Lower extremity loss of hair, brittle nails, pallor, cyanosis, claudication, hypothermia
   → Ulcers are pale to black, well circumscribed and painful, located laterally and distally
2. Diagnosis:
   → Arteriogram is gold standard.
   → Ankle-brachial-index < 0.9
3. Treatment:
   → Definitive treatment: Arterial bypass
   → Medical treatment: Antiplatelets, antilipids, manage risk factors
4. Extremity occlusion: 6 P's- pain, pallor, pulselessness, paresthesias, poikilothermia, paralysis

VARICOSE VEINS

1. Presentation:
   → Lower extremity pain after sitting/standing
   → Dilated tortuous veins
2. Treatment: Compression stockings

VENOUS INSUFFICIENCY

1. Presentation:
   → Edema, atrophic shiny skin, brawny induration. Varicosities.
   → Ulcers above medial malleolus.
2. Treatment: Sclerotherapy, vein stripping, compression hose

VENOUS THROMBOSIS / DVT

1. Physical exam: Homan's sign, lower extremity swelling
2. Risk factors:
   → Virchow's triad: stasis, vascular injury, hypercoagulable state (OCP, cancer, surgery, factor V Leiden)
3. Diagnosis: Duplex ultrasound
4. Treatment: Heparin to Coumadin bridge

SUPERFICIAL THROMBOPHLEBITIS

1. Etiology: Spontaneous or after trauma, or IV/PICC lines
2. Presentation: Dull pain, erythema, induration of vein
3. Treatment: Symptomatic: NSAIDs, warm compress, elevation

CARDIOVASCULAR SYSTEM

VALVULAR DISEASE

1. Diagnostic studies:
   → Make diagnosis with transthoracic echocardiogram / TTE
   → Assess severity with heart catheterization, stress test or transesophageal echocardiogram / TEE
2. Valve Repair:
   → Tissue valve
      * Lasts 10-20 years, indicated for elderly patients
      * No anticoagulation
   → Prosthetic valve
      * Last 20-30 years, indicated for younger patients
      * Requires life long warfarin therapy. INR goal is 2.5-3.5
3. Aortic Stenosis:
   → Population: Elderly, bicuspid valve
   → Symptoms: Syncope, Exertional dyspnea, angina, heart failure
   → Physical exam:
      * Crescendo-Decresendo mid systolic ejection murmur. Radiates to carotids.
      * Paradoxical splitting
   → Treatment: Valve replacement for severe disease
4. Aortic Regurgitation:
   → Popluation: Bicuspid aortic valve, rheumatic heart, endocarditis, marfan disease
   → Symptoms: Syncope, Exertional dyspnea, angina, heart failure
   → Physical Exam:
      * Early diastolic blowing murmur
      * Austin Flint murmumr (low rumbling at apex as blood hits)
      * Quincke's pulse (subungual capillary pulsation)
      * Corrigan (rapid rise and fall of carotid pulse)
      * Laterally displaced PMI
   → Treatment: Valve replacement for severe disease, manage hypertension
5. Mitral Regurgitation:
   → Population: Rheumatic fever, new murmur after MI (papillary muscle rupture), endocarditis
   → Symptoms: Exertional dyspnea, exercise intolerance
   → Physical exam: Holosystolic high-pitched blowing murmur at apex that radiates to axilla
   → Treatment: Definitive- Valve replacement for severe disease
6. Mitral Valve Prolapse:
   → Population: Female or post MI
   → Physical exam: Mid systolic click, audible seated or supine
7. Mitral Stenosis:
   → Symptoms: Exertional dyspnea, exercise intolerance
   → Population: Rheumatic fever
   → Physical exam: Low frequency diastolic rumble located at apex
   → Treatment: Balloon valvuloplasty for severe disease

CARDIOVASCULAR SYSTEM

1. Tricuspid Regurgitation:
   → Symptoms: Asymptomatic or fatigue, edema, ascites, dyspnea
   → Physical exam: Holosystolic murmur at lower left sternal border that radiates to sternum
   → Treatment: Diuretics for symptomatic patients
2. Tricuspid Stenosis:
   → Rarely symptomatic
   → Rarely seen without mitral stenosis
   → Physical exam: Diastolic rumble
3. Pulmonic Regurgitation:
   → Rarely symptomatic
   → Population: Pulmonary hypertension, endocarditis
   → Physical exam: Early diastolic blowing murmur
4. Pulmonic Stenosis:
   → Etiology: Congenital
   → Rarely symptomatic
   → Physical exam: Systolic ejection murmur at pulmonic area that radiates to left neck

PERICARDITIS

1. Presentation: Sharp chest pain, worse leaning forward
2. Physical exam: Pericardial friction rub
3. EKG: Diffuse ST elevation
4. Treatment: Aspirin +/- steroids

PERICARDIAL EFFUSION

1. Fluid in pericardial space ssociated with malignancy, MI, trauma
2. Diagnosis: Echocardiogram
3. Radiograph: Water bottle heart
4. Treatment: Underlying cause, pericardiocentesis if effusion is large

CARDIAC TAMPONADE

1. Physical exam:
   → Beck's triad: Jugular venous distention, hypotension, muffled heart sounds
   → Pulsus paradoxus (drop 10 mmHg in systolic pressure on inspiration), narrow pulse pressure
2. EKG: Electrical Alternans
3. Treatment: Pericardiocentesis

CARDIOVASCULAR SYSTEM

RHEUMATIC HEART DISEASE

1. Organism: Group A streptococcus
2. Jones Criteria
   → Major Criteria
      * Polyarthritis
      * Carditis- new regurgant murmur
      * Subcutaneous nodules
      * Erythema marginatum- evanescent erythematous macular rings on trunks and arms
      * Sydenham's chorea- rapid purposeless movements
   → Minor Criteria
      * Minor Criteria: Fever, arthralgias, elevated ESR, leukocytosis, heart block, previous rheumatic heart disease
3. Treatment: Aspirin or steroids and penicillin

DIGOXIN TOXICITY

1. Yellow-green visual disturbance, EKG changes, nausea, vomiting

INFECTIVE ENDOCARDITIS

1. Duke Criteria:
   → Major:
      * Blood cultures: S. aureus, S. viridins, S. bovis or other typical species times 2, 12 hours apart
        • Drug users: Staphylococcus. Non-drug users: Steptococcus.
      * Echocardiogram: vegetations seen (tricuspid-IV drug users, mitral-nondrug users),
      * New regurgitant murmur
   → Minor: Risk factor, fever 100.5, vascular phenomena (splinter hemorrhages, Janeway lesions: painless, palms and soles), immunologic phenomena (Osler node: raised painful tender; Roth spots: exudative lesions on retina)
2. Treatment:
   → Empiric treatment: IV vancomycin or ampicillin/sulbactam PLUS aminoglycoside *(gentamicin, tobramycin)*
   → Prosthetic valve: Add rifampin
   → High Risk patients prophylaxis for procedures: Amoxicillin

HEMATOLOGY AND ONCOLOGY

IRON DEFICIENCY ANEMIA

1. Most common anemia in the US.
2. Always consider GI bleed.
3. Associated with pica and nail spooning
4. Diagnositic studies:
    → Microcytic Hypochromic anemia
    → Low Ferritin (best test)/Fe, high TIBC
    → Target cells
5. Treatment: FeSO4 325mg TID.
    → Packed red blood cells when Hgb <8.

VITAMIN B12 DEFICIENCY

1. Etiology: Pernicious anemia (antibody to intrinsic factor), gastrectomy, vegans
2. Presentation: Smooth beefy, sore tongue. Neurologic symptoms (poor balance, low proprioception)
3. Diagnostic studies:
    → Megaloblastic anemia. Hypersegmented neutrophils
    → Elevated serum MMA, Elevated homocysteine
    → Pernicious anemia: Schilling test (less than 10% radiolabeled vitamin B12 in urine. Normal results when repeated with administration of intrinsic factor)

FOLIC ACID DEFICIENCY

1. Population: Alcoholics
2. Diagnostic studies:
    → Megaloblastic anemia
    → Elevated homocysteine, normal MMA

ANEMIA OF CHRONIC DISEASE

1. Diagnostic studies: Normochromic/normocytic anemia initially
2. Treatment: Erythropoietin and treat underlying disease

SICKLE CELL ANEMIA

1. Hemolytic anemia
2. Presentation:
    → Population: African Americans. Present 1st year of life.
    → Hemolysis, jaundice, splenomegaly, priapism, poor healing, pain/swelling hands and feet, acute chest syndrome, pigmented gallstones
    → Osteomyelitis with Salmonella
3. Diagnosis: Hemoglobin electrophoresis: Hemoglobin S
    → Blood smear: Sickled RBCs, howell-Jolly bodies, target cells
4. Treatment: Hydroxyurea
    → Vaccine: meningococcal, pneumococcal, H. influenzae, influenza

HEMATOLOGY AND ONCOLOGY

THALASSEMIA

1. Diagnostic studies: Microcytic hypochromic. Elevated iron.
2. Beta thalassemia major
   → Presentation: Most severe, Mediterranean descent, failure to thrive
   → Hemoglobin electrophoresis: Hemoglobin A2 and F
   → Treatment: transfusion dependent. iron chelation (deferoxamine)
3. Beta thalassemia trait
   → Presentation: Mild anemia, often misdiagnosed as iron deficient
   → Hemoglobin electrophoresis: Hemoglobin A2
4. Alpha thalassemia:
   → Population: Chinese and southeast Asians
   → Hemoglobin electrophoresis: Hemoglobin H (H disease), Hemoglobin Barts (hydrops fetalis), Hemoglobin A (trait)

SPHEROCYTOSIS

1. Inheritance: Autosomal dominant
2. Findings: Spherical RBCs, increased MCHC, howell Jolly bodies, positive osmotic fragility test.
3. Treatment: Splenectomy and folate replacement

G6PD DEFICIENCY

1. African, middle eastern, S. Asian population
2. Flare triggers: Fava beans, antimalarials, sulfonamides
3. Diagnostic studies: Heinz bodies. Hemolytic anemia

APLASTIC ANEMIA

1. Diagnostic studies: Pancytopenia

SIDEROBLASTIC ANEMIA

1. Etiology: Lead poisoning
   → Basophilic stippling
2. Diagnostic studies: Prussian blue staining

HEMOPHILIAS

1. Presentation: Spontaneous hemarthrosis
2. Diagnostic studies: Increased PTT
3. Hemophilia A: Factor VIII deficiency
   → Males, 80% of cases
4. Hemophilia B: Factor IX deficiency (Christmas disease)
   → Males, 20%
5. Hemophilia C: Factor XI deficiency (Rosenthal Syndrome)

HEMATOLOGY AND ONCOLOGY

von WILLEBRAND DISEASE

1. Most common inherited bleeding disorder
   → Inheritance: Autosomal dominant
2. Presentation: Nose bleeds, menorrhagia.
3. Diagnostic studies: Elevated PTT, prolonged bleeding time, decreased von Willebrand factor
4. Treatment: Desmopressin
   → Also used for prophylaxis

DISSEMINATED INTRAVASCULAR COAGULATION

1. Etiology: Trauma, sepsis, malignancy.
   → Coagulation factors are used up.
2. Presentation: Simultaneous bleeding and clotting.
3. Diagnostic studies: Prolonged PT, PTT. Low platelets. Elevated D dimer.
4. Treatment: Plasma transfusion, heparin for severe clotting and treatment of underlying cause

HEPARIN INDUCED THROMBOCYTOPENIA

1. Heparin therapy 5-10 days prior
2. Treatment: Supportive and stop heparin
3. Complication: Thrombosis.

THROMBOTIC THROMBOCYTOPENIC PURPURA

1. Cause:
   → After drugs: Quinidine, cyclosporine & pregnancy
   → Inhibition of ADAMTS13
2. Presentation:
   → Adults
   → Purpura and "FAT RN"- Fever, Anemia, Thrombocytopenia, Renal failure, Neurological symptoms
3. Diagnostic studies: CBC normal except low platelets. Schistocytes
4. Treatment: Steroids, plasmapheresis

HEMOLYTIC UREMIC SYNDROME

1. Presentation:
   → Post-infection: E.coli or Shigella
   → Children
   → Severe kidney problems

IMMUNE THROMBOCYTOPENIC PURPURA

1. Diagnosis of exclusion
   → Associated with HIV, HCV, SLE, CLL
   → CBC normal except low platelets
2. Treatment: IVIG or steroids

HEMATOLOGY AND ONCOLOGY

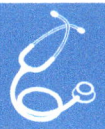

FACTOR V LEIDEN MUTATION

1. Most common hypercoagulable disorder
2. Diagnosis: Activated protein C resistance testing

ACUTE LYMPHOCYTIC LEUKEMIA

- Population: Children
- Diagnostic studies: Philadelphia chromosome indicates poor prognosis

ACUTE MYELOID LEUKEMIA

1. Myelodysplastic syndrome and CML may precede
2. Diagnostic studies
   - Auer rods
   - 20% myeloblasts

CHRONIC LYMPHOCYTIC LEUKEMIA

1. Population: Adults
2. Diagnostic studies: Smudge cells, mature lymphocytes.

CHRONIC MYELOID LEUKEMIA

1. Diagnostic studies: Philadelphia chromosome.
2. Complications: Blast crisis

MULTIPLE MYELOMA

1. Presentation: "CRAB"- Calcium elevation, Renal failure, Anemia Bone lesions
2. Findings:
   - Urinalysis: Bence Jones Protein
   - Blood smear: Rouleaux formation (stacked RBCs)
   - Radiograph: Lytic lesions of skull, spine, long bones
   - Serum/Urine electrophoresis: M protein spike
   - Bone marrow biopsy: > 10% clonal plasma cells

NON HODGKIN'S LYMPHOMA

1. Presentation: Virchow's node lymphadenopathy
2. Most common type: Diffuse large B-cell
3. Burkett's- more often seen in children.
   - Biopsy: "Starry sky pattern"
   - Associated with Epstein-Barr virus

HODGKIN'S LYMPHOMA

1. Biopsy: Reed-Sternberg cells
2. Most common type: Nodular sclerosis
3. Associated with Epstein-Barr virus

HEMATOLOGY AND ONCOLOGY

ANTIDOTES

1. Coumadin: Vitamin K
   → Refractory: fresh frozen plasma
2. Heparin: Protamine sulfate

TUMOR MARKERS

1. CA19-9 Pancreatic CA
2. CA125: Ovarian CA
3. AFP: Liver CA
4. CEA: colon/biliary CA
5. PSA: Prostate

INFECTIOUS DISEASE

ANTIBIOTIC GUIDE

PENICILLINS
- Antibiotics:
  - Penicillin:
    - Treats syphilis, group B strep in pregnant mothers, N. meningidis
  - Aminopenicillins:
    - Antibiotics: Ampicillin, Amoxicillin
    - Treats respiratory tract infections, S. pneumoniae
  - Beta Lactamase Resistant:
    - Antibiotics: Oxacillin, Nafcillin, Dicloxacillin, Cloxacillin
    - Effective against Staphylococcus sp. (Not MRSA), skin infections, osteomyelitis
  - Piperacillin/Tazobactam
    - Pseudomonas sp.
- Gram positive coverage
- Side effects: Rash, GI upset

CEPHALOSPORINS
- 1st Generation:
  - Antibiotics: Cefazolin, Cefadroxil, Cephalexin
  - Use for skin infections and surgery prophylaxis
  - Gram positive coverage
- 2nd Generation:
  - Antibiotics: Cefaclor, Cefuroxime, Cefoxitin
  - Used for intra abdominal infections
  - Gram positive coverage
- 3rd Generation:
  - Antibiotics: Ceftriaxone, Cefdinir, Ceftazidime
  - Gram negative and some gram positive coverage
  - Good CNS penetration, used against N. meningidis
  - Ceftazidime has pseudomonal coverage
- 4th Generation:
  - Cefepime
  - Pseudomonas and gram negative coverage
- Contraindications: anaphylactic reaction to penicillin

QUINOLONES
- Antibiotics:
  - Ciprofloxacin: Urinary tract infections, diarrhea
  - Levofloxacin and Moxifloxacin: Respiratory infections
- Side effects: Tendon rupture, prolonged QT
- Contraindications: Pregnancy, children

INFECTIOUS DISEASE

AMINOGLYCOSIDES
- Antibiotics: Gentamicin, tobramycin, streptomycin
- Coverage: Gram negative, Pseudomonas, Listeria
- Side effects: Ototoxicity, renal failure
- Contraindications: Renal Failure, Pregnancy

TETRACYCLINES
- Antibiotics: Doxycycline, Minocycline, Tetracycline
- Doxycycline treats Rocky Mountain spotted fever, lyme disease, Chlamydia, malaria
- Side effects: Tooth mottling, photosensitivity
- Contraindications: Kids < 8 years old, pregnancy

MACROLIDES
- Antibiotics: Erythromycin, Azithromycin, Clarithromycin
- Coverage: Gram positive, Legionella, Mycoplasma, Mycobacteria, Chlamydia, Haempilus
- Use when patient has allergy to penicillin.
- Often used in pneumonia (esp mycoplasma pneumonia)
- Side effects: Prolonged QT

TRIMETHOPRIM/SULFAMETHOXAZOLE
- Treats UTIs, PCP prophylaxis, Toxoplasmosis
- Side Effects: Steven Johnson Syndrome
- Contraindications: G6PD, allergy

CLINDAMYCIN
- Bone and teeth penetration
- Coverage: Anaerobes
- Often used in toxic shock syndrome, acne
- Side effect: C. difficile

METRONIDAZOLE
- Treats bacterial vaginosis, trichomoniasis, amoebas, giardiasis, C. difficile
- Contraindications: Pregnancy, Alcohol

VANCOMYCIN
- Oral: gut infections (C. difficile)
- Intravenous: MRSA infections

LINEZOLID
- MRSA coverage

INFECTIOUS DISEASE

CARBAPENEMS
- Antibiotics: Imipenem, Meropenem
- Last resort in treatment

IMPORTANT ORGANISMS

1. Pseudomonas:
   - Gram negative aerobicbacillus. May produce color pyocyanin (blue), fluorescein (yellow/green), or pyomelanin (black)
   - More likely in high moisture: hot tubs folliculitis, swimmer's ear, ventilator pneumonia, catheter UTI
   - Antibiotics—aminoglycosides* (gentamicin, tobramycin, amikacin), ceftazidime, cefepime, piperacillin-tazobactam, carbapenem.

1. Staph aureus:
Gram positive cocci in clusters
   - Abscesses, endocarditis, osteomyelitis, septic arthritis, impetigo, HAC pneumonia, surgical infections, sepsis, TSS, scalded skin syndrome
   - Surgical prophylaxis: cefazolin
   - Treatment:
     * MSSA-Penicillinase-resistant penicillin (IE. Dicloxacillin)
     * MRSA- Clindamycin, TMP/SMX, tetracycline, linezolid
       - Severe: Vancomycin

3. Streptococcus pneumoniae:
   - Gram positive "lancet shaped" diplococci or short chains, encapsulated organism
   - Pneumonia, meningitis (adults), otitis media, sinusitis
   - Vaccine for asplenic patients and patients over 65
   - Treatment: Penicillins

4. Streptococcus pyogenes:
   - Group A streptococcus
   - Treatment: Penicillin V or G, clindamycin, macrolide

5. Neisseria meningitides
   - Gram negative diplococci, encapsulated organism, oxidase positive chocolate agar
   - Meningitis, meningococcemia
   - Treatment: Penicillin G, ampicillin, vancomycin, ceftriaxone

6. Neisseria gonorrhoeae
   - Gram negative diplococci
   - Gonorrhea, neonatal conjunctivitis, PID, septic arthritis
   - Treatment: Ceftriaxone or Cefixime.
     * Add azithromycin or doxycycline for Chlamydia coverage

7. Escherichia coli
   - Gram negative rods
   - UTI, sepsis, neonatal meningitis, travelers diarrhea
   - Treatment:
     * UTI- Nitrofurantoin, TMP/SMX, Fosfomycin.
       - Complicated: Ciprofloxacin

INFECTIOUS DISEASE

* Meningitis/sepsis- 3rd generation cephalosporin

8. Clostridium Difficile:
   → Treatment: Metronidazole, Vancomycin
9. Moraxella Catarrhalis:
   → Treatment: Cefuroxime

DIPHTHERIA

1. Presentation: URI with thick gray pseudomembrane in throat in someone who wasn't vaccinated.
2. Treatment: Antitoxin and antibiotic (penicillin or macrolide)

BOTULISM

1. Gram positive
2. Presentation: Flaccid paralysis and respiratory, "floppy babies"
3. Etiology: Honey. (No honey for babies)
4. Treatment: Botulinum antitoxin

TETANUS

1. Gram positive.
   → Neurotoxin.
   → Transmission: Rusty nail
2. Presentation: First symptom is pain and tingling at site. Later muscle spasms and respiratory muscle tetany
3. Treatment: Immunoglobulin, wound debridement and penicillin
4. Prognosis: High mortality

GONORRHEA

1. Gram negative diplococci
2. Presentation:
   → Women: Asymptomatic.
   → Men: Purulent discharge
3. Treatment: Ceftriaxone IM, cefixime PO once + Azithromycin/doxycycline for chlamydia coverage
4. Complications:
   → Disseminated: fever, joint pain, skin lesions, pericarditis, meningitis
   → Septic arthritis

CHLAMYDIA

1. Gram negative rod. Intracellular
2. Most common STD
3. Asymptomatic, dysuria
4. Diagnosis: NAAT.
   → Gram stain reveals no organisms
5. Treatment: azithromycin once, doxycycline PO x 7 days

INFECTIOUS DISEASE

SYPHILIS

1. Treponema pallidum – gram negative spirochetes.
2. Presentation:
   → Stage 1: Chancre- painless
   → Stage 2: Macules palms and soles
   → Stage 3: Neuro symptoms: Argyll Robertson pupils (accommodate, not react). Tabes Dorsalis (ataxia, lighting pains, urinary incontinence)
3. Diagnosis: RPR and VDRL. Confirm with antibody testing
4. Treatment: Benzathine Penicillin or penicillin G.

HAEMOPHILUS DUCREYI

1. Chancroid- painful genital ulcer

BORRELIA/ LYME DISEASE

1. Borrelia burgdorferi: deer tick transmition.
2. Symptoms:
   → First manifestation: Erythema migrans (target lesions)
   → Arthritis, Bell's palsy, CNS symptoms
3. Diagnosis: IFA or ELISA
4. Treatment: Doxycycline
   → < 8 years old, treat with amoxicillin
   → Do not treat if tick exposure is known to be <24 hours

RICKETTSIA RICKETTSII/ ROCKY MOUNTAIN SPOTTED FEVER

1. Gram negative spirochete
   → Transmission: Wood or dog tick bite.
   → Endemic area: Southeast US
2. Presentation: Fever, disseminated macular rash, delerium
3. Treatment: Doxycycline

VARICELLA/CHICKENPOX

1. Diagnosis: Positive Tzanck smear

HIV

1. Highest transmission rate- anoreceptive intercourse
2. Diagnosis: ELISA, confirm with western blot. PCR amplification to test for exposure (not enough time to develop antibodies)
3. Treatment: 3 Antiretroviral medications.
   → TwoNucleoside Reverse Transcriptase Inhibitors
   → PLUS oneNon-Nucleoside Reverse Transcriptase Inhibitor, Protease Inhibitor OR Integrase Inhibitor

INFECTIOUS DISEASE

AIDS

1. HIV infection and CD4 count below 200 or opportunistic infection:
   - Candida
   - HSV
   - Herpes Zoster
   - Hairy leukoplakia
     - Epstein-Barr virus, white lesions on lateral tongue, cannot be scraped off
   - Kaposi's sarcoma
     - Red/purple plaques
     - Caused by Human Herpesvirus 8
   - Tuberculosis
   - Pneumocystis pneumonia
     - Prophylaxis with Bactrim
   - Coccidioidomycosis
   - Histoplasmosis
     - Bird/bat droppings, soil
     - Dyspnea, fever
   - Progressive multifocal leukoencephalopathy
     - Focal neurological deficits
     - Nonenhancing white matter lesions
   - Toxoplasmosis
     - T. gondii
       - Transmission: cats
     - Head CT: Multiple lesions on basal ganglia and thalamus
     - Treatment: Pyrimethamine and folic acid
   - Cryptosporidium
     - Drinking water. Watery diarrhea
   - Cryptococcosis
     - Meningitis. India ink staining
     - Treatment: Fluconazole +/- amphotericin B
   - Mycobacterium Avium Complex:
     - Very common. Fever, diarrhea, weight loss, anemia
   - Cytomegalovirus
     - Symptoms:
       - Most common: retinitis (neovascularization)
       - Esophagitis, GI symptoms, pulmonary symptoms, neurological symptoms
     - Tissue biopsy: Intracytoplasmic inclusions
     - Treatment: Ganciclovir
   - Cervical Cancer
   - Lymphoma
   - Muscle wasting syndrome
     - Chronic fatigue, 10% loss of muscle

INFECTIOUS DISEASE

RABIES
1. Transmission: raccoons, skunks, bats, fox, coyote
2. Post exposure treatment: Rabies immunoglobulin and 5 series of Rabies vaccine (day 0, 3, 7, 14, 30)
3. Prognosis: Fatal when there are neurological symptoms

MALARIA
1. Organism: Plasmodium spp.
2. Transmission: mosquitos
3. Peripheral smear: see parasites
4. Treatment: Chloroquine

AMEBIASIS
1. Entamoeba histolytica
2. Common symptom: colitis
3. Stool culture: trophozoites and cysts
4. Treatment: metronidazole and amebicide

HOOKWORMS
1. Stool culture: Eggs
2. Treatment: Albendazole or Mebendazole

PINWORMS
1. Symptoms: Anal pruritis
2. Scotch tape test: see eggs or worms
3. Treatment: Albendazole or Mebendazole

GENITOURINARY

BENIGN PROSTATIC HYPERPLASIA

1. Enlargement of transitional zone
2. Treatment:
   - Symptomatic: Alpha blocker (Tamsulosin)
   - Decrease prostate size: 5 alpha reductase inhibitors (Finasteride)
   - Definitive: TURP

CRYPTORCHIDISM

1. Risk of malignancy and infertility
2. Treatment: Orchiopexy by age 1

HYDROCELE

1. Physical exam: Mass will transilluminate

VARICOCELE

1. Dilation of the pampiniform plexus
2. Presentation:
   - "Bag of worms" on testicular palpation
   - More common on left

TESTICULAR TORSION

1. Presentation:
   - Teenage males
   - Very tender to palpation. Cremaster reflex absent.
   - "Blue dot sign"
2. Diagnosis: Radionucleotide study and ultrasound
3. Treatment: Surgical emergency. Repair both testes within 4-6 hours

PARAPHIMOSIS

1. Entrapment of the foreskin behind glans
2. More acute than phimosis

GENITOURINARY

PHIMOSIS

1. Unable to retract foreskin
2. More chronic than paraphimosis

ERECTILE DYSFUNCTION

1. Consider psychological cause
2. Treatment: PDE5s
   → Cannot take with Nitroglycerin

INCONTINENCE

1. Stress- cough, sneeze, laugh, lift. Cystocele. Incompetent sphincter. Vaginal delivery.
   → Treatment: strengthen pelvic floor or surgery
2. Urge- frequency. Vaginal delivery.
   → Treatment: Oxybutynin
3. Overflow- Cannot empty bladder, just leaks. High PVR.
   → Treatment: Self catheterization.
4. Functional- mobility issue
5. Total- anatomic issue.
   → Treatment: surgical

UROLITHIASIS

1. Types:
   → Calcium oxalate-Excess oxalate, hyperparathyroidism
      * Most common
   → Uric Acid- Excess meat/alcohol, gout.
   → Struvite- Associated with UTI with Klebsiella and Proteus spp
   → Cystine- Rare genetic
2. Presentation: Flank pain radiate to groin. Hematuria. CVA tenderness
3. Treatment
   → Lithotripsy - Stones > 1 cm unlikely to pass.
   → Hydration- Stones < 5 mm likely to pass.

CYSTITIS

1. Organism: E. coli
2. Treatment: Bactrim, Nitrofurantoin (not over age 65), Fosfomycin
   → Pregnant patient receives nitrofurantoin.
   → Ciprofloxacin- reserved for complicated cases
3. Interstitial cystitis –Symptoms relieved with void. Diagnosis of exclusion.
   → "Hunner's ulcer" on cystoscopy

GENITOURINARY

EPIDIDYMITIS/ORCHITIS

1. Presentation: Painful swelling of scrotum
2. Physical exam: Phren's sign- pain relief with elevation of scrotum
3. Orchititis- rarely seen without epididymitis unless patient has mumps
4. Organism:
    - Over 35- E. coli.
        * Treatment: Ciprofloxacin
    - Under 35 – Gonorrhea and chlamydia
        * Treatment: Ceftriaxone and doxycycline/azithromycin

PROSTATITIS

1. Population: Young men
2. Physical exam: No prostate massage
3. Treatment: Ciprofloxacin or sulfamethoxazole/trimethoprim

URETHRITIS

1. Diagnosis: NAAT testing
2. Organisms:
    - N. gonorrhea (gram negative diplococci)
        * Treatment: Ceftriaxone + Azithromycin (co tx for chlamydia)
    - C. trachomatis
        * Treatment: Azithromycin or Doxycycline

PYELONEPHRITIS

1. Organism: E. coli
2. Presentation: Irritative voiding, fever, CVA tenderness
3. Urinalysis: Bacteria and WBC casts
4. Treatment:
    - Outpatient: Sulfamethoxazole/trimethoprim or ciprofloxacin
    - Inpatient: Ciprofloxacin or ampicillin + gentamicin

BLADDER CANCER

1. Risk Factors: Smokers
2. Most common type: Transitional cell cancer
3. Presentation: Painless hematuria

PROSTATE CANCER

1. Most common area: Peripheral zone
2. Tumor marker: PSA. (also elevated in BPH)
3. Digital Rectal Exam: hard, irregular, nodular prostate

GENITOURINARY

TESTICULAR CANCER

1. Most common type: seminoma
2. Presentation: Painless testicular mass
   → History of cryptorchidism
3. Diagnostic studies:
   → Initial- Ultrasound
   → Tumor markers: AFP, hCG

RENAL CELL CARCINOMA

1. Risk factors: Smoking, von Hippel Lindau
2. Presentation
   → Triad: hematuria, flank pain, palpable mass

WILM'S TUMOR

1. Children with unilateral renal mass

ACUTE RENAL FAILURE

1. Pre-renal:
   → Most common
   → Etiology: Volume depletion, CHF, cirrhosis, renal artery stenosis, nephritic syndrome
   → Diagnostic studies: BUN/Cr ratio > 20:1. Fractional urine excretion of sodium <1%
2. Intrinsic Renal:
   → Etiology: Acute tubular necrosis, nephrotoxins, glomerulonephritis, interstitial nephritis, vascular diseases
   → Diagnostic studies: BUN/Cr ratio < 15:1. Fractional urine excretion of sodium >2%
      * Presence of casts, proteinuria
3. Post-renal:
   → Etiology: Obstruction- BPH, tumors, calculi

CHRONIC KIDNEY DISEASE

1. Etiology: Diabetes, hypertension, glomerulonephritis
2. Findings: Fatigue, pruritus, Kussmaul respirations, asterixis (flapping tremor), muscle wasting, broad waxy casts
3. Stages:
   → Stage 1: GFR > 90 mL/min
      * asymptomatic
   → Stage 2: GFR 60-89
      * asymptomatic
   → Stage 3: GFR 30-59
   → Stage 4: GFR 15-29
      * Dialysis and kidney transplant
   → Stage 5: GFR < 15
      * Kidney transplant

GENITOURINARY

GLOMERULONEPHRITIS

1. Presentation/Findings:
   → Oliguria, hematuria, proteinuria, hypertension, RBC casts
2. Etiology:
   → Kids - Previous streptococcal infection
   → Adults- SLE, Goodpasture's, IgA nephropathy
3. Treatment: Steroids, symptomatic treatment

NEPHRITIC SYNDROME

1. Urinalysis: 1-2 g protein in 24 hours

NEPHROTIC SYNDROME

1. Urinalysis: >350 mg protein in 24 hours, Oval fat bodies

INTERSTITIAL KIDNEY DISEASE

1. Urinalysis: WBC casts and eosinophils

ACUTE TUBULAR NECROSIS

1. Etiology: Kidney ischemia or toxins
2. Urinalysis: Muddy brown casts

HYDRONEPHRITIS

1. Urine outflow obstruction causes renal distention

POLYCYSTIC KIDNEY DISEASE

1. Autosomal dominant
2. Presentation: Back, flank pain
3. Ultrasound: Many fluid filled cysts
4. Treatment: Supportive

FLUID AND ELECTROLYTE DISORDERS

1. Hypernatremia:
   → Etiology: Diarrhea, burns, diuretics, hyperglycemia, diabetes insipidus, deficit of thirst
   → Rapid overcorrection causes cerebral edema and pontine herniation
2. Hyponatremia:
   → Presentation: Muscle cramps and seizures
   → Etiology:
      * Hypervolemia – CHF, nephrotic syndrome, renal failure, cirrhosis
      * Euvolemia – SIADH, steroids, hypothyroid
      * Hypovolemia – sodium loss (renal, non-renal)
3. Hyperkalemia
   → Presentation: Peaked T waves prolonged QRS, muscle fatigue

GENITOURINARY

- → Treatment: Insulin, sodium bicarbonate and glucose. (drive potassium back into cell). Calcium gluconate (antagonize effect of potassium on heart)
4. Hypokalemia
   - → Presentation: muscle cramps, constipation, flattened/inverted T waves, U waves
5. Hypercalcemia-
   - → Presentation: "Stones, bones, abdominal groans, psychiatric moans"
   - → Associated with malignancy and hyperparathyroidism.
   - → Treatment: IV normal saline and furosemide
6. Hypocalcemia-
   - → Presentation: QT prolongation, Trousseau's sign, Chvostek's sign
   - → Treatment: IV calcium gluconate or calcium chloride
7. Hyperphosphatemia:
   - → Etiology: CKD
   - → Treatment: calcium carbonate, restrict potassium
8. Hypophosphatemia:
   - → Usually asymptomatic
9. Hypermagnesemia:
   - → Presentation: Muscle weakness, prolonged QT, PR and wide QRS
   - → Treatment: IV calcium gluconate, saline and furosemide
10. Hypomagnesemia:
    - → Presentation: Muscle weakness, hyperreflexia, prolonged QT, PR and wide QRS, ventricular tachycardia, torsades de pointes
    - → Treatment: IV magnesium sulfate (acute) or oral magnesium oxide (chronic)

ACID/BASE DISORDERS:

1. Average values: "24/7 40/40"
   - → 24 (HCO_3, base) / 7.40 (pH) / 40 (CO_2, acid)

RESPIRATORY ACIDOSIS:

1. pH < 7.35, pCO_2 > 45, HCO_3 > 26
2. Lungs fail to excrete CO_2 (pulmonary disease, neuromuscular disease, drug induced hypoventilation)

RESPIRATORY ALKALOSIS:

1. pH > 7.45, pCO_2 < 35, HCO_3 < 22
2. Excessive elimination of CO_2 (anxiety, salicylate intoxication, septicemia)

METABOLIC ACIDOSIS:

1. pH <7.35, pCO_2 < 35, HCO_3 < 22
2. Addition of hydrogen ions (lactic acidosis, diabetic ketoacidosis)
   - → Increased ion gap. (Na – (HCO_3 + Cl)) = 8 +/- 4
3. Loss of bicarbonate (diarrhea, pancreatic or biliary drainage, renal tubular acidosis)

GENITOURINARY

METABOLIC ALKALOSIS
1. pH > 7.45, pCO2 > 45, HCO3 > 26
2. Loss of hydrogen (vomiting), addition of bicarbonate (hyperalimentation therapy), excessive loss of chloride (diarrhea)

NEUROLOGY

MENINGITIS
1. Presentation: Fever, headache, stiff neck, petechiae (especially N. meningitidis)
2. Physical exam:
    → Kernig sign- knee flexion causes pain in neck
    → Brudzinski sign- leg raise when bend neck
3. Bacterial:
    → Etiology:
        * Neonate: E. coli (gram negative rods) and S. agalactiae (Group B Streptococcus)
        * Most people: S. pneumoniae (gram positive diplococci), N. meningitidis (gram negative diplococci)
        * Immunocompromised: Cryptococcus neoformans (Diagnosis: India ink stain)
    → Spinal tap: Increased opening pressure, decreased glucose, increased WBC (neutrophils), increased protein
    → Treatment: Dexamethasone + Empiric IV antibiotics (Cephalosporin, Vancomycin, Penicillins)
4. Aseptic:
    → Etiology: Enterovirus, HSV, TB, fungus
    → Spinal tap- normal pressure, increased WBC (lymphocytes)
    → Treatment: symptomatic or IV acyclovir for HSV

ENCEPHALITIS
1. Etiology:
    → Usually viral
    → Most common species: HSV
    → Immunocompromised: CMV
2. Symptoms: Altered mental status, seizures, personality changes, exanthema
    → Encephalitis is clinically differentiated from meningitis by altered brain functioning
3. Diagnosis: PCR for viruses
4. Treatment: Symptomatic
    → HSV- Acyclovir

BRAIN ABSCESS
1. Organisms: Polymicrobial. Often streptococcus
    → May be toxoplasmosis (many lesions)
2. Presentation: Fever, HA, focal neurological deficits
3. CT or MRI with contrast: Ring enhancing lesion
4. Treatment: CT-guided stereotactic surgical drainage and IV antibiotics (ceftriaxone + metronidazole)

MIGRAINES
1. Presentation:
    → Teens, female
    → Unilateral, throbbing, nausea, vomiting, photophobia
        * Classic: Aura
        * Common: No aura. 80% of migraines
2. Treatment:
    → Abortive: Triptans (do not use in ischemic heart disease), ergotamine (do not use in pregnant women)

NEUROLOGY

→ Prophylaxis: Atenolol, propranolol or verapamil

CLUSTER

1. Presentation: Severe, unilateral, periorbital, lacrimation, nasal congestion
2. Treatment: 100% oxygen

TENSION HEADACHE

1. Presentation: Bilateral, squeezing sensation
2. Treatment: NSAIDs, muscle relaxer

SUBARACHNOID HEMORRHAGE

1. Etiology: Aneurysm or AVM rupture
2. Presentation: Thunderclap headache. "worst headache of my life"
3. Diagnostic studies:
   → Emergent CT
   → Cerebral angiogram is definitive
4. Treatment: Admit, symptomatic treatment, nimodipine for vasospasm control

SUBDURAL HEMATOMA

1. Etiology: Car accident, elderly, alcoholics, shaken baby syndrome
2. Presentation: May be chronic, taking days to weeks to develop symptoms.

EPIDURAL HEMATOMA

1. Presentation: Loss of consciousness, period of lucency, then neurologic deterioration

PSEUDOTUMOR CEREBRI

1. Elevated ICP. Papilledema
2. Presentation: Female, obese
3. Diagnosis:
   → Initial- CT (rule out mass lesion)
   → Then, Lumbar puncture (elevated opening pressure)
4. Treatment: Serial spinal taps, shunt placement

TRIGEMINAL NEURALGIA

1. Presentation: Unilateral face pain. Worse with chewing, smiling etc.
2. Treatment: Carbamazepine (side effects: Agranulocytosis and liver toxicity)

ISCHEMIC STROKE

1. Treatment: Thrombolytics (t-Pa) within 3 hours
2. Middle Cerebral Artery: Most likely affected
   → Contralateral hemiparesis, hemianesthesia, contralateral hemianopsia, gaze preference to affected side
   → Arm and face symptoms > leg symptoms

NEUROLOGY

- → Left side: Aphasia
    - ✱ Wernicke's- receptive aphasia. Word salad.
    - ✱ Broca's- expressive aphasia. Non-fluent speech.
    - ✱ Right side: Apraxia, hemineglect
3. Anterior cerebral artery: Leg symptoms > arm symptoms
4. Posterior cerebral artery: Contralateral visual field loss, affects consciousness
5. Vertebrobasilar artery: Vertigo, CN deficit
6. Lacunar infarct: No impairment. small vessel disease. Risk of vascular dementia.

HEMORRHAGIC STROKE

1. Same presentation as ischemic stroke. Never use thrombolytics
2. Diagnostic studies:
    - → Emergent Head CT
    - → Perform angiogram for ruptured aneurysm

TRANSIENT ISCHEMIC ATTACK

1. Symptoms last less than 24 hours
2. Work up for stroke

DIABETIC NEUROPATHY

1. Presentation: Symmetrical, stocking and glove distribution, postural hypotension
2. Treatment:
    - → Amitriptyline, gabapentin, pregabalin.
    - → Glycemic control.
3. Complications: Charcot's joints

CARPAL TUNNEL

1. Median nerve compression
2. Presentation: 1st and 2nd digit numbness and tingling. Thenar atrophy.
3. Physical exam:
    - → Tinel's: Tap over median nerve causes tingling
    - → Phalen's: Flex hands with dorsal surfaces together for 60 seconds causes tingling
4. Treatment: Wrist splint, NSAIDs
    - → Carpal tunnel release surgery for refractory cases

CUBITAL TUNNEL SYNDROME

1. Ulnar nerve compression
2. Presentation: 4th and 5th digit numbness and tingling. Hypothenar atrophy
3. Physical exam: Tinel's sign at elbow.
4. Treatment: NSAIDs, ulnar nerve release

GUILLAIN-BARRE SYNDROME

1. Presentation:

NEUROLOGY

- → Following Campylobacter jejuni infection
- → Weakness begins in lower extremities
2. Treatment: Admit. plasmaphoresis or IVIG.
    - → Respiratory paralysis if no treatment. Good prognosis

BELL'S PALSY
1. Facial nerve affected (CN VII)
    - → Associated with HSV
2. Presentation: Difficulty with eye closure, eating. Cannot raise eyebrow.
3. Treatment: None or steroids +/- acyclovir.

COMPLEX REGIONAL PAIN SYNDROME
1. Idiopathic
2. Presentation:
    - → Following trauma, injury
    - → Extremity pain and atleast 1 other sensory, motor, vasomotor, edema, sudomotor symptom
3. Treatment: Early physical therapy

ESSENTIAL TREMOR
1. Population: Family history, autosomal dominant. Elderly patients
2. Presentation:
    - → Worse on intention. Hands and head.
    - → Better with alcohol
3. Treatment: Propranolol

PARKINSON'S DISEASE
1. Pathology:
    - → Decreased dopamine in substantia nigra.
    - → Lewy bodies
    - → Acetylcholine/Dopamine imbalance
2. Presentation: Resting/pill rolling tremor, masked facies, cogwheel rigidity, bradykinesia, shuffling gait
3. Treatment: carbidopa, levodopa. Anticholinergics: benztropine
    - → Refractory: Bromocriptine
    - → Adjunct: MAOI-B: selegiline, COMT inhibitors

HUNTINGTON'S DISEASE
1. Population: 40 years old, family history (autosomal dominant inheritance)
2. Presentation: Dementia, chorea
3. Diagnosis:
    - → Genetic testing: 40+ CAG repeats
    - → Imaging: Atrophy of caudate nucleus
4. Treatment: No cure. Tetrabenazine (depletes dopamine)
5. Prognosis: Fatal in 15-20 years

NEUROLOGY

MYASTHENIA GRAVIS

1. Etiology: Autoimmune
2. Presentation:
   → Young women, older men
   → Weakness eye muscles, improves with rest.
3. Diagnosis:
   → Acetylcholine receptor antibodies
   → Tensilon test/edrophonium test- short acting anti-cholinesterase
4. Treatment: cholinesterase inhibitors (pyridostigmine, neostigmine), thymectomy

DEMENTIA

1. Impairment in at least 2 areas of functioning: language, memory, spatial skills, emotional behavior, personality, cognition.

ALZHEIMER'S DISEASE

1. Most common.
2. Definitive diagnosis on autopsy
   → Beta amyloid plaques and neurofibrillary tangles
3. Physical exam: Abnormal clock drawing test
4. Treatment: Anticholinesterase drugs (Tacrine, Donepezil)

VASCULAR DEMENTIA

1. Multi-infarct.
2. Treatment: Blood pressure control

FRONTOTEMPORAL DEMENTIA

1. Personality changes precede memory changes.

LEWY BODY DEMENTIA

1. Parkinsonian symptoms

DELIRIUM

1. Presentation: Acute, fluctuating mental status change
2. Underlying organic cause: UTI, pneumonia, metabolic changes, CVA, MI, TBI, medications (anticholinergics, benzodiazepines, opioids)
3. Treatment: Treat underlying cause

SEIZURES

1. Generalized convulsive:
   → Presentation: Loss of consciousness, increased muscle tone (tonic), jerking muscles (clonic).
   → Postictal phase- confusion after seizure.
   → Treatment: Valproic acid, carbamazepine

NEUROLOGY

2. Absence seizure:
    → Presentation: Children. Blank stare.
    → Treatment: Valproic acid, ethosuximide (only for absence)
3. Simple partial:
    → Presentation: No alteration in consciousness. Abnormal movements or sensations.
    → Treatment: Carbamazepine
4. Complex partial seizure:
    → Presentation: Altered consciousness, automatisms (ie. Lip smacking)
    → Treatment: Carbamazepine
5. Febrile seizure:
    → Treatment: Acetaminophen
6. Status epilepticus
    → Duration >5 minutes, treat.
    → Treatment: IV lorazepam, diazepam
7. Todd's paralysis:
    → Presentation: Brief paralysis after seizure. Subsides after 48 hrs.
8. Other causes:
    → Withdrawal
    → Medications: cocaine, amphetamine, alcohol, phenothiazines (antiemetic), lithium, isoniazid, salicylates, theophylline
    → Infection
    → Metabolic: hypocalcemia, hypomagnesemia, hyponatremia, hypoxia, hypoglycemia

BRAIN TUMORS

1. Most common primary: glioma
2. Most aggressive: glioblastoma multiforme

MULTIPLE SCLEROSIS

1. Autoimmune: Antibodies against myelin sheath.
2. Types:
    → Relapsing remitting (symptoms come and go)
    → Secondary progressive (relapsing remitting progresses to steady decline)
    → Primary progressive (no remission, steady decline from onset)
    → Progressive relapsing (combination. Worse overtime with acute relapses. Most rare.)
3. Often first finding: Retrobulbar optic neuritis.
    → Other symptoms: numbness, tingling, balance disturbance, diplopia
4. MRI: Dawson fingers (white matter lesions)
5. CSF: Elevated IgG, oligoclonal bands
6. Treatment:
    → Acute- steroids
    → Prevent relapses- beta interferon

NEUROLOGY

CEREBRAL PALSY

1. Etiology: Prenatal injury. Preterm baby.
2. Presentation: Hyperreflexia, rigidity, intellectual impairment, seizures
3. Treatment: Supportive

NORMAL PRESSURE HYDROCEPHALUS

1. Presentation: Dementia, ataxic gait, urinary incontinence (urgency, hyperreflexia).
    → "Wet, wobbly, wacky"
2. Diagnosis:
    → CT/MRI to rule out mass lesion, see enlarged ventricles
    → Lumbar puncture- high volume (30-66 cc) or prolonged drainage (3-5 days), which causes clinical improvement in patient
3. Treatment: Ventriculoperitoneal shunt.

BROWN SEQUARD SYNDROME

1. Presentation: Ipsilateral loss of position, motor, vibration. Contralateral loss of pain and temperature.

RADICULOPATHY

1. Typically impinges nerve below disc (ie: L4-L5 herniation causes L5 radiculopathy)
2. C5- bicep reflex
3. C6- brachioradialis reflex
4. C7- triceps reflex
5. L4- patellar reflex
6. L5- pain top of foot/big toe. Weakness- dorsiflexion and great toe
7. S1- Achilles reflex. Pain lateral foot/sole

GLASGOW COMA SCALE:

1. Eye opening:
    → 4- spontaneous
    → 3- voice
    → 2-pain
    → 1-none
2. Verbal:
    → 5-oriented
    → 4-confused
    → 3-inappropriate words
    → 2-incomprehensible
    → 1-none
3. Motor:
    → 6-obeys commands
    → 5-localizes pain
    → 4-withdraws
    → 3-abnormal flexion (decorticate)

NEUROLOGY

- → 2-abnormal extension (decerebate)
- → 1-none

4. Less than 9 is a coma

NEXUS CRITERIA

1. Indications to image the C spine after trauma:
   - → Midline C-spine tenderness
   - → Altered mental status
   - → Intoxication
   - → Abnormal neurological exam
   - → Painful distracting injury

ENDOCRINE

HYPERPARATHYROID
1. Etiology: Parathyroid adenoma
2. Presentation: "stones, bones, abdominal groans, psych moans, fatigue overtones"
   → Nephrolithiasis, DI, bone pain, arthralgia, PUD, constipation, depression, fatigue
3. Labs: Hypercalcemia, hypophosphatemia, elevated iPTH, moderately elevated urinary calcium
4. Treatment:
   → Acute- Saline, calcitonin, bisphosphonates
   → Definitive- Surgical correction. Remove overactive parathyroid gland. If all 4, remove 3.5 glands.

HYPOPARATHYROID
1. Etiology: Thyroidectomy.
2. Presentation: Tetany, cataracts
3. Physical exam:
   → Chvostek's sign (tap facial nerve illicit cheek twitch)
   → Trousseau's sign (BP cuff inflation illicit carpal spasm)
4. Labs: Hypocalcemia, low iPTH, hyperphosphatemia, low urinary calcium
5. Treatment: Vitamin D and Calcium
   → Tetany- secure airway, IV calcium gluconate

HYPERTHYROIDISM
1. Etiology: Grave's disease (autoimmune). Toxic adenoma, thyroiditis, pregnancy, amiodarone
2. Presentation: Heat intolerance, palpitations, sweating, weight loss, tremor, anxiety
   → Graves- Diffuse goiter with a bruit, exophthalmos, pretibial myxedema
   → Thyroid storm- Fever, tachycardia, delirium
3. Diagnosis:
   → TSH (best test): Decreased in primary disease, elevated in secondary disease
   → T4: Elevated
   → Thyroid radioactive iodine uptake:
      * Graves: Diffusely high uptake
      * Toxic multinodular: Discrete areas of high uptake
   → Antibodies:
      * Graves: Anti-thyrotropin antibodies
4. Treatment:
   → Beta blockers (symptomatic), methimazole/propylthiouracil, radioactive iodine, thyroidectomy
   → Thyroid storm- prompt beta blockers, hydrocortisone, methimazole/propylthiouracil, iodine
   → Thyroidectomy- most likely complication is recurrent laryngeal nerve (hoarseness)

HYPOTHYROIDISM
1. Etiology: Hashimoto's (chronic lymphocytic/autoimmune), previous thyroidectomy/iodine ablation, congenital
2. Presentation:
   → Cold intolerance, fatigue, constipation, depression, bradycardia
   → Congenital: round face, large tongue, hernia, delayed milestones, poor feeding

ENDOCRINE

1. Labs: TSH- elevated in primary disease. Low T4
   → Hashimoto's- Antithyroid peroxidase, antithyroglobulin antibodies
2. Treatment: Levothyroxine. Follow up with serial TSH monitoring

THYROID CANCER

1. Most often papillary carcinoma
2. Diagnostic studies:
   → Normal thyroid function. Solitary hard, cold nodule
   → Fine needle biopsy for definitive diagnosis
3. Treatment: Surgical resection

THYROIDITIS

1. Hashimoto's thyroiditis:
   → Diffusely enlarged, nodular goiter
2. Subacute thyroiditis:
   → Young women, viral cause
   → Painful enlarged thyroid with dysphagia, mild fever
   → Treatment: Aspirin
3. Postpartum thyroiditis:
   → 1-2 months of hyperthyroidism after delivery
   → Treatment: Completely resolves, give propranolol for cardiac symptoms
4. Suppurative:
   → Fever, pain, redness, fluctuant mass
   → Treatment: Antibiotic/surgical drainage

CORTICOADRENAL INSUFFICIENCY/ADDISON'S DISEASE

1. Etiology: Typically autoimmune. May be due to Tuberculosis in endemic areas
2. Nonspecific symptoms: Hyperpigmentation, hypotension, fatigue, myalgias, GI complaints
3. Lab Findings:
   → Low sodium, low 8AM cortisol, high ACTH (primary), low ACTH (secondary), high potassium (primary), low DHEA
4. Diagnosis: Cosyntropin test (synthetic ACTH) – cortisol raise in < 20 mcg/dL in primary disease
5. Treatment: Hydrocortisone/prednisone PO daily
   → Crisis: Hypotension, altered mental status.
     * Treatment: Emergent IV saline, glucose, steroids

CUSHING'S DISEASE/SYNDROME

1. Classification:
   → Disease- excess ACTH from pituitary adenoma
   → Syndrome- excess cortisol generally from Cushing disease or excess glucocorticoids
2. Presentation:
   → Fat redistribution (buffalo hump, moon facies, supraclavicular fat), thin hair, hypertension, thin skin, easy bruising, elevated glucose, infections, cataracts, hirsutism, striae

PANCE/PANRE Study Guide

ENDOCRINE

3. Diagnosis: Urine cortisol excretion of > 125 mg/dL in 24 hrs
4. Treatment: Resection of pituitary tumor

PHEOCHROMOCYTOMA

1. Adrenal neoplasm
2. Presentation: Recurrent headaches, HTN, sweating, palpitations.
3. Diagnosis: 24 hour urine catecholamines and metanephrines
4. Treatment:
   → Resect tumor
   → Medical treatment preoperative: Alpha blocker (phenoxybenzamine) + alpha male

ACROMEGALY

1. Etiology: Pituitary adenoma. Excess growth hormone
2. Presentation:
   → Large hands, feet, nose, lips, ears, jaw, tongue
   → Presents as gigantism (excessive height) if occurs before epiphysis close
3. Diagnosis:
   → GH test 2 hour after glucose load
   → Increased IGF-1
   → MRI/CT shows pituitary tumor
4. Treatment: Pituitary tumor removal

DWARFISM

1. Etiology: Achondroplasia (FGFR3 mutation)
2. Presentation: Short stature/limbs, prominent brow, mid facial hypoplasia
3. Treatment: PRN orthopedic surgery

PITUITARY ADENOMA

1. Size:
   → Microadenoma- <10mm
   → Macroadenoma >10mm
2. Type:
   → Prolactinoma:
     * Most common
     * Secrete prolactin
     * Presentation: Galactorrhea, infertility, amenorrhea
     * Treatment: Bromocriptine
   → Somatotrophic:
     * Secret GH
     * Presentation: Acromegaly
     * Treatment: Resection is first line
   → Corticotrophic:
     * Secrete ACTH

ENDOCRINE

- * Presentation: Cushing syndrome
- * Treatment: Resection
→ Gonadotrophic:
- * Rare
- * Secrete LH and FSH
- * Treatment: Resection
→ Thyrotrophic:
- * Secrete TSH
- * Presentation: Hyperthyroidism
- * Treatment: Resection
→ Null cell:
- * No secretion

HORNER'S SYNDROME

1. Presentation: Unilateral ptosis, anhidrosis, miosis (constriction)

DIABETES TYPE 1

1. Etiology: Autoimmune- HLA-DR3/4/O antibodies. Islet cell antibodies
2. Presentation:
   → Children
   → Weight loss, polydipsia, polyuria
   → Often first recognized as diabetic ketoacidosis:
   - * Symptoms: Fruity breath, nausea, vomiting, dehydration
   - * Treatment: IV regular insulin
3. Treatment: Insulin

DIABETES TYPE 2

1. Diagnosis: random glucose >200 x2. Fasting glucose >126 x 2
2. Treatment:
   → Metformin
   - * Side effects: Lactic acidosis, GI side effects
   → Sulfonylureas
   - * Glyburide, glipizide, glimepiride
   - * Side effects: Hypoglycemia
   → Thiazolidinediones
   - * Pioglitazone
   - * Contraindications: CHF, liver disease
   → Alpha glucosidase inhibitors
   - * Acarbose, miglitol
   - * GI side effects
   → Incretins
   - * DDP4- sitagliptin, Incretin mimetics-Exenatide
   - * Side effects: Hypoglycemia, severe allergy

ENDOCRINE

- Insulin –add if HbA1C >9
1. Follow Up: Annual- opthamologist visit, urine microalbumin
2. Complications –neuropathy (most common), retinopathy (leading cause of blindness), nephropathy

SOMOGYI EFFECT
1. Hypoglycemia at night, rebound hyperglycemia in morning
2. Treatment: Reduce insulin at night

DAWN PHENOMENON
1. Only hyperglycemia at 4-8 AM
2. Treatment: Long acting insulin at bed time

DIABETES INSIPIDUS
1. Types:
   - Central –Deficiency of ADH from posterior pituitary/hypothalamus
   - Nephrogenic – Lack of reaction to ADH
2. Diagnosis:
   - 24 hr urine –specific gravity 1.006
   - Vasopressin challenge test (central DI)
3. Treatment:
   - Central – desmopressin
   - Nephrogenic— indomethacin +/- HCTZ, desmopressin
     NSAID

SIADH
1. Euvolemic hyponatremia

HYPERLIPIDEMIA
1. Subcutaneous xanthomas, premature arcus senilis, lipemia retinalis
2. Medications:
   - Statins
     * Side effects: Elevated LFTs, myalgias
   - Fibrates
     * Side effects: Gallstones
   - Niacin
     * Side effects: Flushing
   - Bile acid sequestrants (Ie. Cholestyramine)
     * Side effects: Diarrhea
3. Treatment Guidelines:

ENDOCRINE

Population	LDL Goal	Treatment Indicated when LDL is
0-1 Risk Factors for CAD	<160	190
2 or More Risk Factors for CAD	<100	130
CAD	<70	100

DERMATOLOGY

TERMINOLOGY

1. Papule – raised, solid <10 mm
2. Nodule – raised, solid >10 mm
3. Macule – flat <10 mm
4. Patch – flat >10 mm
5. Plaque – plateau-like >10 mm
6. Vesicle – raised, contains serous fluid <5 mm
7. Bulla – raised, contains serous fluid >5 mm
8. Pustule – raised, contains purulent material
9. Wheal – elevated lesion from local edema, transient
10. Crust – hard surface, dried sebum, exudates, blood, necrotic skin
11. Scale – horny epithelium with dry appearance
12. Erosion – defect of epidermis (non scarring)
13. Ulcer – defect of dermis or deeper (scarring)

DERMATITIS

1. Contact dermatitis:
   → Allergic:
      * Etiology: Nickel, poison ivy etc.
         - Type 4 hypersensitivity
   → Irritant (diaper rash):
      * Etiology: Cleaners, solvents, detergents, urine, feces
   → Presentation: Well demarcated erythema, erosions, vesicles
   → Treatment: Avoid offending agent. Burrow's solution (aluminum acetate), topical steroids, zinc oxide (diaper rash)
2. Atopic dermatitis:
   * Presentation: Pruritic papules and plaques
   * Etiology: IgE, type 1 hypersensitivity
   * Location:
      - Infant- face and scalp.
      - Adolescent- flexural surfaces
3. Nummular eczema:
   → Presentation: Coin shaped/discoid plaques
4. Seborrheric dermatits (cradle cap):
   * Presentation: Erythematous/yellow, scaly crusted lesions.
   * Location:
      - Infants- scalp
      - Adults/adolescents- body folds
   → Treatment: Ketoconazole shampoo
5. Perioral dermatitis:
   → Presentation: Young women. Papulopustules, plaques and scales around mouth.
   → Treatment: Topical metronidazole, avoid steroids

DERMATOLOGY

DYSHIDROSIS

1. Presentation: Tapioca vesicles on hands and feet following stress or hot humid weather
2. Treatment: Topical steroids

LICHEN SIMPLEX CHRONICUS

1. Long term manifestation of scratching atopic dermatitis
2. Presentation: Thick plaques
3. Treatment: Break the itch-scratch cycle (anti-histamines, occlusive dressing)

LICHEN PLANUS

1. Presentation:
    - 5 P's: purple, papule, polygonal, pruritis, planar
    - Wickham striae
2. Treatment: Topical steroids

PITYRIASIS ROSEA

1. Presentation:
    - Herald patch: Large oval plaque with central clearing and scaly border. 1st sign
    - Pruritic erythematous plaque with central scale in Christmas tree pattern on trunk
2. Disease is self limiting

PSORIASIS

1. Presentation: Erythematous plaque with silver scaling
2. Types:
    - Psoriasis vulgaris- most common. Noted on extensor surfaces
    - Guttate- children. After URI. Small lesions
    - Inverse- intertriginous areas.
    - Pustular- contains pustules
3. Signs:
    - Auspitz sign (bleeds when scale is picked)
    - Koebner's phenomenon (minor trauma causes new lesion)
4. Treatment: Topical steriods

ERYTHEMA MULTIFORME

1. Etiology: HSV, sulfa drugs
2. Presentation: Target lesions on hands, feet and mucosa
3. Treatment: Avoid trigger

STEVEN JOHNSON SYNDROME/ TOXIC EPIDERMAL NECROLYSIS

1. SJS is 3-10% of body, TEN is > 30% of body
2. Etiology: drug reaction- most often sulfa drugs. Also other antibiotics, anti-epileptics
3. Presentation: Prodrome, then morbiliform lesions, blisters, necrotic epidermis, Nikolsky sign (pushing

DERMATOLOGY

blister causes further separation from dermis)
4. Diagnosis:
   → Biopsy- shows necrotic epithelium
5. Treatment: Treat underlying cause and supportive (burn unit)

PEMPHIGUS VULGARIS

1. Etiology: Autoimmune disease
2. Presentation:
   → Vesicles and bullae on oral mucosa and skin
   → Nikolsky's sign
   → Only epidermal layer and more fragile than bullous pemphigoid.

BULLOUS PEMPHIGOID

1. Etiology: Autoimmune disease
2. Presentation:
   → Large bullae and crusts located on axillae, thighs, groin, abdomen
   → More tense, less fragile and deeper than pemphigus vulgaris
3. Treatment: Systemic steroids

ACNE VULGARIS

1. Presentation: Open comedones (blackheads), closed comedones (whiteheads), papules, pustules, nodules or cysts
2. Treatment:
   → Most acne- topical retinoids
   → Cystic acne- tetracyclines, then oral retinoids- isotretinoin (causes dry lips, liver damage, pregnancy category X)

ROSACEA

1. Presentation:
   → Women aged 30-50
   → Facial erythema, telangiectasias, papules
   → Triggers: heat, alcohol, spicy foods
2. Treatment: metronidazole topical

ACTINIC KERATOSIS

1. Presentation: Flesh colored, pink or yellow-brown lesion with rough sandpaper feel at sun exposed areas
2. Treatment: Cryotherapy, electrodessication
   → May progress to squamous cell carcinoma

SEBORRHEIC KERATOSIS

1. Presentation: Brown-black stuck on waxy plaques
2. Treatment: Unnecessary. Excise for cosmetics

DERMATOLOGY

LICE (PEDICULOSIS)

1. Presentation:
    → Pruritic scalp, body or groin.
    → Nits are observed as small white specs on hair shaft
2. Treatment: Permethrin

SCABIES

1. Presentation: Pruritic papules. S shaped or linear burrows on skin. Often located in web spaces
2. Diagnosis: Microscopic observation of mite, egg or feces after skin scrape
3. Treatment: Permethrin

SPIDER BITES

1. Brown recluse- necrotic wound
2. Black widow- neurologic manifestation (muscle ache, spasm, rigidity)

BASAL CELL CARCINOMA

1. Presentation: Raised pearly borders, telangiectasis, central ulcer (Rodent ulcer)
2. Treatment: Excise with clear margins

SQUAMOUS CELL CARCINOMA

1. Presentation: Hyperkeratotic macule, scaling
2. Treatment: Excise with clear margins

MELANOMA

1. ABCDE: Asymmetry, Border is irregular, Color variability (blue, red, white), Diameter (> 6 mm), Evolution

KAPOSI'S SARCOMA

1. Presentation: Violaceouspapular lesions associated with AIDs
2. Caused by Human Herpesvirus 8

ALOPECIA

1. Alopecia areata:
    → Presentation: Oval shaped well demarcated hair loss
    → Etiology: Autoimmune
    → Treatment: Clobetasol
2. Androgenetic alopecia (male pattern baldness)
    → Location: Top of head
3. Telogen effluvium
    → Presentation: Diffuse hair loss that occurs after stress, illness, medication
    → Treatment: Self limiting
4. Traction alopecia
    → Etiology: Tight hairstyles

DERMATOLOGY

ONYCHOMYCOSIS
1. Presentation: Thick, yellow, brittle nails
2. Treatment: Oral terbinafine

PARONYCHIA
1. Inflammation around nail
2. Organism: Staphylococcus sp
3. Treatment: Warm soaks, drain visible pus, anti-staph antibiotic

CONDYLOMA ACUMINATUM (GENITAL WARTS)
1. Etiology: HPV Types 6 and 11
2. Presentation: Flesh colored, cauliflower appearance

EXANTHEMS
1. Measles(Rubeola)
   - Etiology: Measles virus
   - Presentation: Koplik spots (grains of sand on erythematous base), cough, coryza, conjunctivitis, cephalocaudal spread of maculopapular rash
2. Rubella (German Measles)
   - Etiology: Rubella virus
   - Presentation: 3 days. Cephalocaudal spread of maculopapular rash, lymphadenopathy
   - Teratogenic in pregnancy (worst outcomes in first trimester)
3. Roseola
   - Etiology: Human Herpesvirus 6 or 7
   - Presentation: Fever, then subsequent macular rash beginning on trunk
4. Erythema Infectiosum / Fifth disease
   - Etiology: Parvovirus B19
   - Presentation: Slapped cheek with lace-like rash
5. Hand-foot-mouth:
   - Etiology: Coxsackie virus.
   - Presentation: Children<10 years old with vesicles on pharynx, mouth, hands, feet

HERPES SIMPLEX
1. Presentation: Grouped vesicles on erythematous base all at the same stage of development
2. Types: HSV 1- Oral lesions, HSV 2 - Genital lesions
3. Treatment: Manage flares with acyclovir

MOLLUSCUM CONTAGIOSUM
1. Etiology: Poxvirus
2. Presentation: Pearly papule with umbilicated center

VARICELLA ZOSTER VIRUS
1. Chicken pox-
   - Presenation: Vesicular lesions in different stages of development. "Dew drop on rose petal"

DERMATOLOGY

2. Shingles-
    → Presentation: Pain precedes rash in dermatomal pattern
    → Hutchinson's sign- lesion on nose. Concern for eye involvement

VERRUCAE

1. Etiology: HPV
2. Types:
    → Verruca vulgaris- skin colored papillomatous papules. Hands
    → Verruca plana- flat warts. Face, arms, legs
    → Plantar warts- bottom of foot. Rough surface. Dark spot (thrombosed capillaries)

CELLULITIS

1. Presentation: Warm erythematous tender skin with induration or fluctuance
2. Organism: Staphylococcus aureus is most common
3. Treatment: Dicloxacillin

ERYSIPELAS

1. Presentation: Distinct sharp, raised, demarcated border, more superficial than cellulitis. Fever, chills.
2. Organism: Group A streptococcus
3. Treatment: Dicloxacillin

IMPETIGO

1. Organism: Staphylococcus aureus is most common
2. Presentation:
    → Nonbullous- Honey colored crusts around nose and mouth.
    → Bullous- thin walled vesicles
3. Treatment: Mupirocin ointment

CANDIDIASIS

1. Presentation: Beefy red plaques with satellite lesions
2. Location: Groin in infants, under breast folds in adults
3. Treatment: Nystatin cream. Ketoconazole for refractory cases.

DERMATOPHYTE

1. Tinea pedis (foot), tinea cruris (groin), tinea corporis (body), tinea barbae (beard area), tinea capitis (head)
    → Organism: Trichophyton
    → Presentation: Annular erythematous patch with scaly borders and central clearing. Pruritus
    → KOH prep: Segmented hyphae and spores
    → Treatment: Topical ketoconazole
2. Tinea versicolor:
    → Organism: Malassezia furfur
    → Presentation: Hypo or hyper pigmented macules on upper trunk.

DERMATOLOGY

- → KOH prep: Curved hyphae and spores, "spaghetti and meatballs"
- → Treatment: Ketoconazole shampoo

ACANTHOSIS NIGRICANS

- → Presentation: Thick velvety hyperpigmentation and accentuated skin lines around neck, armpits, groin
- → Associated with insulin resistance

BURNS

1. Body percentage:
   - → Rule of 9's: Head 9% Each arm 9%, Chest 9%, Abdomen 9%, Each anterior leg 9%, Each posterior leg 9%, Upper back 9%, Lower back 9%, Genitals 1%
   - → Palmar method: Patient's palm equates to 1%
2. Degree involvement:
   - → First degree- erythema, tenderness
   - → Second degree (partial thickness)- blisters
   - → Third degree (full thickness)- white, leathery, charred skin
   - → Fourth degree- bone or muscle involvement
3. Treatment: Monitor ABCs, fluid replacement, sulfadiazine

HIDRADENITIS SUPPURATIVA

1. Presentation: Tender nodules or abscesses in axilla and groin

LIPOMAS/EPITHELIAL INCLUSION CYSTS

1. Benign adipose tumors.
2. Treatment: Can be removed for cosmetic reasons

MELASMA/CHLOASMA/MASK OF PREGNANCY

1. Presentation:
   - → Hyperpigmented macules in sun exposed areas.
   - → Associated with pregnancy

PILONIDAL DISEASE

1. Presentation: Abscess in sacrococcygeal cleft
2. Treatment: Surgical drainage

PRESSURE ULCERS/DECUBITUS ULCERS

1. Location: Sacrum and hip most often affected
2. Prevention: Reposition every 2 hours
3. Treatment: Debridement

URTICARIA

1. Presentation: Pruritic erythematous wheal

DERMATOLOGY

VITILIGO

1. Presentation: Depigmented macules
2. Diagnosis: bright blue under wood's lamp

HENOCH-SCHONLEIN PURPURA

1. Presentation:
   - Often follows infection
   - Palpable purpura, often on legs

FOLLICULITIS

1. Organisms:
   - After shaving- Staphylococcus aureus
   - After hot tub- Pseudomonas aeruginosa

NEUROFIBROMATOSIS

1. Type 1 is most common
2. Presentation:
   - 6+ Café au lait patches
     - \>5 mm before puberty, >15 mm after puberty
   - 2+ Neurofibromas (rubbery skin nodules)
   - Crowe's sign (axillary freckling)
   - 2+ Lisch nodules (pigmented iris hamartomas)

SCARLET FEVER

1. Presentation: Fever, pharyngitis, strawberry tongue, sandpaper rash on trunk, desquamating rash on palms and soles
2. Organism: Group A Streptococcus

KAWASAKI DISEASE

1. Population: Children
2. Presentation: High fever, 5 day rash, conjunctivitis, cracked lips, strawberry tongue, cardiovascular complications (myocarditis, pericarditis, arteritis, aneurysms)

RHEUMATIC FEVER

1. Presentation: Erythema marginatum
2. Organism: Group A Streptococcus

PSYCHIATRY

GENERALIZED ANXIETY DISORDER

1. Excessive worry most days for 6 months or more
2. Treatment: SSRIs

PANIC DISORDER

1. Acute attacks of anxiety
2. Anxiety about having another attack
3. With or without agoraphobia (fear of situations that would be difficult to escape)
4. Treatment:
   → Chronic: SSRIs
   → Acute: benzodiazepines

PHOBIAS

1. Persistent fear and avoidance of object/situation
2. Treatment: cognitive behavioral therapy

POST-TRAUMATIC STRESS DISORDER

1. Traumatic event (rape, car accident, combat), flashbacks, avoidance, significant distress
2. Symptoms > 1 month

ACUTE STRESS REACTION

1. PTSD symptoms for less than 1 month

ATTENTION DEFICIT/HYPERACTIVITY DISORDER

1. Inattention and hyperactivity/impulsivity for 6 months
2. Present before age 7, in 2 or more settings
3. Treatment: Stimulants (methylphenidate, mixed amphetamine salts)

AUTISTIC DISORDER

1. Developmental delay in socialization, language and cognition

ANOREXIA NERVOSA

1. 85% of expected weight, amenorrhea
2. Treatment: Cognitive behavioral therapy, weight gain, SSRIs

BULIMIA NERVOSA

1. Recurrent binging and purging (vomiting, laxative use, exercise) 2 times weekly for 3 months
2. Russell's sign (calluses on knuckles of dominant hand), eroded enamel
3. Treatment: Cognitive behavioral therapy, SSRIs

OBESITY

1. BMI > 30 (BMI = lbs x 703/ in2)

PSYCHIATRY

ADJUSTMENT DISORDER

1. Behavioral/emotional symptoms in response to stressor within 3 months of stressor

BIPOLAR DISORDER

1. Type 1: At least 1 manic or mixed episode, may or may not alternate with depression
   - Manic episode –
     * Symptoms: 3 or more "DIG FAST"- Distractibility, Insomnia, Grandiosity, Flight of ideas, Agitation, Speech, Taking risks
     * Causes significant impairment
     * At least 1 week duration or causes hospitalization
   - Mixed episode –
     * Manic and major depressive episodes alternating nearly every day for 1 week
2. Type 2: At least 1 episode of major depression and at least 1 episode of hypomania
   - Hypomania –
     * 3 or more "DIG FAST" symptoms, but does not cause marked impairment in functioning
   - Major Depression –
     * Symptoms: 5 or more "SIG E CAPS"- sleep disturbance, Interest loss, Guilt, Energy changes, Concentration loss, Appetite changes, Psychomotor changes, Suicidal thoughts
3. Treatment:
   - Lithium
     * Risk of nephrotoxicity and thyroid toxicity. Must monitor lithium levels.
   - Valproate, carbamazepine, lamotrigine
   - SSRIs may cause manic episode

MAJOR DEPRESSIVE DISORDER

1. Symptoms: 5 or more "SIG E CAPS"- Sleep disturbance, Interest loss, Guilt, Energy changes, Concentration loss, Appetite changes, Psychomotor changes, Suicidal thoughts
2. At least 2 weeks duration
3. Causes significant dysfunction
4. Treatment: *Prozac   Zoloft   Celexa   Paxil*
   - SSRIs (Fluoxetine, Sertraline, Citalopram, Paroxetine)
     * Risk of serotonin syndrome (hyperthermia, muscle rigidity, altered mental status)
   - SNRIs (Venlafaxine, Duloxetine)
   - TCAs (Amitriptyline, Nortriptyline)
     * Anticholinergic side effects.
     * Risk of cardiovascular toxicity. (Treat with Sodium bicarbonate)
   - MAOIs
     * Cannot eat foods with tyramine (cheese, wine), risk of Hypertensive crisis
   - Mirtazapine
     * Sedation and increased appetite- good for elderly
   - Bupropion /*Wellbutrin*
     * Risk of seizures

PSYCHIATRY

DYSTHYMIC DISORDER
1. Depressed mood on most days that persists for more than 2 years.
2. No symptom free interval > 2 months

CYCLOTHYMIC DISORDER
1. Periods of hypomania and periods of depression symptoms for 2 years.
2. No symptoms free intervals > 2 months

PERSONALITY DISORDERS
1. Cluster A (mad)
    - Schizoid – social isolation, detached
    - Schizotypal – magical thinking, strange behavior/dress
    - Paranoid – distrustful, suspicious
2. Cluster B (bad)
    - Borderline – unstable relationships, self mutilation, fear of abandonment
    - Histrionic – desire to be center of attention, promiscuous
    - Narcissistic – grandiose sense of self importance
    - Antisocial – criminals
3. Cluster C (sad)
    - Avoidant – shy, fear criticism
    - Dependent – submissive, clingy
    - Obsessive compulsive – preoccupation with cleanliness (unlike OCD, OCPD is not aware of illness)

DELUSIONAL DISORDER
1. Erotomanic- believe someone is in love with individual
2. Grandiose- believe inflated self worth or fame
3. Jealous- believe partner is unfaithful
4. Persecutory- believe individual has been drugged or spied on etc.
5. Somatic- believe individual has physical defect

SCHIZOPHRENIA
1. Major types:
    - Paranoid – delusions, auditory hallucinations
    - Disorganized – difficult to understand speech/behavior, inappropriate or flatted emotions
    - Catatonic – difficulty moving, abnormal posture
    - Residual – Negative symptoms only (flattened affect, social withdrawal, avolition (loss of motivation), alogia (loss of speech))
2. Symptoms persistent for 6 months
    - If not,
        * 1 month- 6 months = Schizophreniform disorder
        * 1 day- 1 month = Brief psychotic disorder
3. Treatment:
    - Antipsychotics:

PSYCHIATRY

- Typical- Chlorpromazine (Thorazine), Haloperidol (Haldol).
    - Side effects: Extrapyramidal side effects and tardive dyskinesia
- Atypical- Olanzapine (Zyprexa), Risperidone (Risperdal)
- Clonidine- risk of agranulocytosis
- Risk of neuroleptic malignant syndrome (fever, muscle rigidity, altered mental status, autonomic dysfunction)
→ Negative symptoms are most difficult to treat

SOMATOFORM DISORDERS

1. Conversion disorder:
   → Neurologic complaints that cannot be explained clinically + serious precipitating emotional event
2. Somatization disorder:
   → 4 pain symptoms, 2 gastrointestinal symptoms, 1 sexual symptom, 1 pseudo-neurological symptom
3. Pain disorder:
   → Significant distress over pain without identifiable cause
4. Hypochondriasis:
   → Fear and preoccupation with disease
5. Malingering:
   → Feigning illness for secondary gain (compensation, drugs)
6. Factitious disorder/Munchausen:
   → Feigning illness to obtain the sick role

SUBSTANCE USE

1. Substances:
   → Marijuana: Red, glassy eyes
   → Depressants (alcohol, benzodiazepines): Miosis (constricted pupils), clumsiness
       - Treat alcohol withdrawal with benzodiazepines to avoid seizures
       - Disulfiram- causes severe nausea when consumed with alcohol
       - Benzodiazepine overdose: Flumazenil
   → Stimulants (amphetamines, cocaine): Mydriasis (dilated pupils), hyperactivity, dry mouth
   → Hallucinogens (LSD, PCP): Mydriasis, paranoia
   → Opioids/Heroin: Miosis, stupor, respiratory depression
       - Antidote- Naloxone (Narcan)
2. Classification:
   → Abuse- substance use resulting in functional impairment
   → Physical Dependence- withdrawal symptoms, when not using substance
   → Psychological dependence- craving of substance

CHILD ABUSE

1. Injury inconsistent with history, delayed reporting
2. Burns in stocking-glove distribution, symmetrically round (cigarettes)
3. Retinal hemorrhages (shaken baby syndrome)

PSYCHIATRY

CONDUCT DISORDER
1. Aggression towards people/animals/property, deceit, rule violation
2. Develop anti-social personality disorder as an adult

GRIEF REACTION
1. Normal grief symptoms resolve in 1 year, most severe symptoms resolve in 2 months

REPRODUCTIVE

DYSFUNCTIONAL UTERINE BLEEDING

1. Symptoms: Polymenorrhea, menorrhagia and/or metrorrhagia
2. Diagnosis of exclusion
3. Treatment: Oral contraceptives and NSAIDs

ENDOMETRIAL CANCER

1. Presentation: Post menopausal vaginal bleeding
2. Most often adenocarcinoma
3. Diagnosis: Endometrial biopsy
4. Treatment: Hysterectomy bilateral salpingo-oophorectomy +/- radiation

ENDOMETRIOSIS

1. Symptoms: Dysmenorrhea, dyspareunia, dyschezia, infertility
2. Signs: Uterus is fixed and retroflexed. Tender nodularity of cul de sac and uterine ligaments.
3. Laparoscopy: Chocolate cysts observed. Definitive study.
4. Treatment: Resect endometriosis, oral contraceptive therapy

LEIOMYOMA (UTERINE FIBROIDS)

1. Presentation:
    - Symptoms: Polymenorrhea, menorrhagia, intermenstrual bleeding and/or metrorrhagia. Uterine mass.
    - Population: Black women, family history
2. Ultrasound: Uterine mass
3. Intramural fibroids are most common
4. Treatment:
    - Symptomatic medical treatment: NSAIDs, OCPs, Danazol, Leuprolide (also used to shrink fibroids pre-operatively)
    - Definitive: myomectomy or hysterectomy

ADENOMYOSIS

1. Symptom: Dysmenorrhea
2. Sign: Boggy uterus
3. Ultrasound: Subendometrial linear striations
4. Treatment:
    - NSAIDs and hormones.
    - Hysterectomy is definitive treatment

OVARIAN TORSION

1. Sudden onset abdominal pain, fever, leukocytosis
2. May be due to ovarian mass
3. Treatment: Emergent surgery. Untwist ovary (remove, if necrotic)

REPRODUCTIVE

OVARIAN CYST

1. Pain, menstrual delay, hemorrhagic shock from cyst rupture
2. Follicular cysts are most common
3. Ultrasound: Observe cyst
4. Treatment:
   → Most resolve in 1 month.
   → Persistent cysts, large cysts or complex cysts can be removed

POLYCYSTIC OVARIAN SYNDROME

1. Presentation: Overweight, menstrual irregularities, hirsutism, diabetes mellitus
2. Ultrasound: String of pearls
3. Treatment: Oral contraceptives, metformin

OVARIAN CANCER

1. Population: 40-60 years of age.
2. Symptoms: Ascites, abdominal pain
3. Tumor marker: CA 125

CERVICAL DYSPLASIA/CANCER

1. Etiology: HPV especially types 16, 18. Associated with cigarette smoking
2. Transformational zone most commonly affected
3. Gardasil vaccine at age 11-12
4. Pap smear every 3 years starting at age 21
   → Every 5 years if pap smear and HPV are negative starting at age 30
5. ASC-US or LSIL, CIN-1
   → Reflex HPV
     * If positive and at least 25 years old – colposcopy
     * If negative or under 25 years old – retest in 1 year
6. HSIL, CIN-2, CIN-3, CIS
   → Colposcopy
     * Outside cervix – LEEP or cryotherapy
     * Inside cervix – cone biopsy
7. Squamous cell carcinoma
   → Treatment: Resect and/or chemotherapy and radiation

CERVICITIS

1. Etiology: Gonorrhea and/or Chlamydia
2. Sign: Cervical motion tenderness.
3. Treatment: Ceftriaxone for gonorrhea + Azithromycin for Chlamydia

INCOMPETENT CERVIX

1. Etiology: History of cone biopsy, DES exposure
2. Can lead to miscarriage or preterm birth

REPRODUCTIVE

3. Only treated if threatens pregnancy
- → Cervical cerclage (suture cervix)

♥ VULVAR CANCER

1. Squamous cell and melanoma – pruritic black lesions
- → Treatment: Vulvectomy and lymph node dissection

2. Paget's – pruritic red lesions
- → Treatment: Local resection

♥ VAGINAL CANCER

1. Squamous cell carcinoma – caused by HPV
2. Adenocarcinoma – caused by DES exposure

♥ PELVIC ORGAN PROLAPSE

1. Presentation:
- → Caucasian women, after labor/delivery, chronic cough
- → Vaginal fullness, abdominal pain worse late in day, after prolonged standing. Relieved by lying down.

2. 0- No descent, 1- descent between normal and ischial spine. 2- between ischial spines and hymen. 3-within hymen. 4- through hymen.

3. Location:
- → Anterior- cystocele
  - ✱ Stress incontinence
  - ✱ Treatment: kegel exercises, pessary or surgical replacement
- → Apical- vaginal vault, urterovaginal prolapse
- → Posterior- rectocele

♥ VAGINITIS

1. Trichomonas:
- → Signs: Frothy yellow, green, gray vaginal discharge and strawberry cervix
- → Wet mount: Flagellated protozoa
- → pH: Basic
- → Treatment: Metronidazole

2. Bacterial vaginosis:
- → Organism: Haemophilus aka Gardnerella
- → Signs: Fishy odor, thin gray discharge
- → Wet mount: Clue cells
- → pH: Basic
- → Treatment: Metronidazole

3. Candida
- → Signs: Thick white vaginal discharge
- → Associated with recent antibiotic use, diabetes mellitus, steroid use
- → KOH prep: Pseudohyphae
- → pH: Normal (4)
- → Treatment: Fluconazole

REPRODUCTIVE

AMENORRHEA

1. Primary- no menses by age 16
   → Turner's syndrome – XO karyotype, webbed neck, broad chest
   → Androgen insensitivity – breast development only
   → Imperforate hymen – observed on speculum exam
   → Mullerian agenesis – secondary sex characteristics, no uterus
2. Secondary- previously had menses, amenorrhea for 6 months
   → Most often pregnancy
   → Also caused by weight changes, hypothyroid, prolactinoma

DYSMENORRHEA

1. Primary:
   → Treatment: NSAIDs and oral contraceptive pills
2. Secondary:
   → Etiology: Adenomyosis, endometriosis, fibroid, PID, IUD
   → Treat underlying cause

PREMENSTRUAL SYNDROME

1. Presentation:
   → Symptoms during luteal phase (1-2 weeks before menses)
   → Bloating, irritability
2. PMDD- causes marked disruption in functioning

MENOPAUSE

1. 12 months without a period
2. Average age is 51.5
3. Definitive diagnosis: FSH > 30 mIU/mL

BREAST CANCER

1. Most common malignancy in women
2. Risk factors (increased exposure to estrogen):
   * Menarche before age 12
   * Old age of first full term pregnancy, no pregnancies
   * Menopause after age 52
3. Breast mass- immobile, irregular
4. Nipple retraction, bloody nipple discharge

FIBROADENOMA

1. Presentation:
   → Young adult female with rubbery, firm, well circumscribed, mobile, non-tender breast mass.
   → No changes with menstrual cycle

REPRODUCTIVE

FIBROCYSTIC DISEASE

1. Presentation:
   → Multiple bilateral breast masses that increase in size and pain before menses
   → Aspiration of cysts- straw colored fluid

GYNECOMASTIA

1. Affects pubescent boys
   → Treatment: Watch and wait. Typically resolved in 1 year.
2. Klinefelter's syndrome- XXY karyotype, tall, thin, long limbs
3. Hypogonadism.
   → Treatment: Danazol

GALACTORRHEA

1. Symptoms: Milky white nipple discharge
2. Rule out pituitary adenoma

MASTITIS

1. Population: Breastfeeding mothers
2. Organism: S. aureus
3. Treatment: Dicloxacillin, warm compresses. Continue to breastfeed.

BREAST ABSCESS

1. Complication of mastitis
2. Treatment: Drainage

PELVIC INFLAMMATORY DISEASE

1. Etiology: Gonorrhea, Chlamydia, IUD
2. Signs: Chandelier sign (cervical motion tenderness)
3. Complications: infertility, ectopic pregnancy, tubo-ovarian abscess (adnexal mass)

CONTRACEPTION

1. Barrier method:
   → Condoms- prevent STDs
2. Oral contraceptive pills
   → Combined estrogen and progesterone- not used in women > 35 years of age that are smokers, patients with history of blood clots, breast cancer or migraines with aura
   → Progestin only pill- used by breastfeeding mothers
3. Intrauterine Devices:
   → Most effective form of birth control. Reversible.
   → Copper IUD- women who cannot have hormones that want children later in life
4. Irreversible forms:
   → Tubal litigation, transcervical sterilization, vasectomy (in men)

REPRODUCTIVE

INFERTILITY

1. Failure to conceive after 1 year of unprotected intercourse
2. First step: Test male sperm
3. Treatment for anovulatory women: Clomiphene citrate

UNCOMPLICATED PREGNANCY

1. G_ P_ or G_ P _ _ _ _
   → G is number of pregnancies
   → P is number of deliveries
   → OR P is full-term deliveries, premature deliveries, abortions, living children
2. Nagel's rule for due date: LMP + 7 days – 3 months
3. Chadwick's sign- blue cervix. Hagal's sign- cervical softening
4. First trimester (weeks 1-12)
   → Fetal heart tones: 10-12 weeks
   → Screening:
      * PAPP-A
      * Free beta HCG
      * Nuchal translucency- ultrasound (10-13 weeks)
         • >3.5 mm – trisomy or neural tube defect
      * CVS (10-13 weeks)
5. Second trimester (weeks 13-27)
   → Fetal movement:
      * Nullipara: 18-20 weeks
      * Multipara: 14-16 weeks
   → Uterine growth
      * At umbilicus – 20 weeks
      * Weeks gestation should equal fundal height in cm
   → Screening:
      * Maternal AFP
         • Increased- neural tube defects
         • Decreased- trisomy
      * Inhibin A
      * Unconjugated estriol
      * Ultrasound (18-20 weeks)
         • anatomy scan, gender reveal
      * Amniocentesis (15-18 weeks)
6. Third trimester (weeks 28- birth)
   → Full term is 37 weeks. Plan for induction after 40 weeks.
   → Vaccines:
      * Tdap (28 weeks)
      * Rhogam (28 weeks) – for Rh negative mothers only
   → Screening:
      * Gestational diabetes (24-28 weeks)

REPRODUCTIVE

- Rh antibodies for Rh negative mothers (28 weeks)
- Vaginal-rectal culture for Group B strep (35 weeks)
  - If positive, treat with IV penicillin during delivery
- Nonstress test
  - 20 minute monitoring, should see two accelerations (15 BPM above baseline, for 15 seconds), and no decelerations
- Biophysical profile
  - NST, amniotic fluid level, fetal movements, fetal tone, fetal breathing

7. Labor and Delivery
   → Cervical examination:
     - Dilation – up to 10 cm
     - Effacement (softening) – up to 100%
     - Station (position of baby head) – 0 is at ischial spine.
   → Stages of labor:
     - 1- Onset contractions to full dilation (primi- 6-20 hours) (multi- 2-14 hours)
     - 2- Full dilation to baby delivery (primi- 30 mins-3 hours) (multi- 5-6 minutes)
     - 3- After baby delivery to expulsion of placenta (0-30 mins)
       - Placenta should have 2 arteries and 1 vein
   → APGAR score:
     - Activity (2=active movement), Pulse (2= >100 BPM), Grimace (2= pulls away, sneeze), Appearance (2=pink), Respiration (2=crying)
     - Score > 6 is good. Score of 4 necessitates resuscitation.

ABORTION

1. Threatened – vaginal bleeding, closed cervical os
2. Inevitable – vaginal bleeding, open cervical os, no passage of tissue
3. Incomplete – vaginal bleeding and tissue passage from open cervical os
4. Complete – complete passage of fetal tissue

ABRUPTIO PLACENTAE

1. Presenation: Heavy painful vaginal bleed in 3rd trimester
2. Treatment: C-section

PLACENTA PREVIA

1. Presenation: Heavy painless vaginal bleed in 3rd trimester
2. Treatment: C-section

CESAREAN SECTION

1. Indications: previous C-section, dystocia, breech presentation, fetal distress

DYSTOCIA

1. Failure of cervical dilation and fetal descent
2. Causes:

REPRODUCTIVE

- → Small pelvis
- → Poor contractions
  - ✱ Treatment: IV pitocin
- → Macrosomia
3. Treatment: Forceps, vacuum, C-section

ECTOPIC PREGNANCY

1. Most often in ampulla
2. Ultrasound:
   - → Ring of fire sign.
   - → Beta HCG is > 1,500, but no fetus in utero
3. Treatment:
   - → Salpingostomy
   - → Salpingectomy if rupture
   - → Methotrexate:
     - ✱ Only if beta HCG < 5,000, ectopic mass is < 3.5 cm, no fetal heart tones, no folate supplements

GESTATIONAL DIABETES

1. Most common complication: macrosomia
2. Oral glucose tolerance testing
   - → 24-28 weeks gestation- 50 g 1 hr challenge.
     - ✱ Positive if blood glucose is > 130 mg/dL
   - → Confirmatory test- 100g 3 hr challenge.
     - ✱ Need two positive values for diagnosis.
       - Fasting glucose > 95 mg/dL
       - One hour > 180 mg/dL
       - Two hour >155 mg/dL
       - Three hour > 140 mg/dL
3. Treatment: Dietary modification and insulin

GESTATIONAL TROPHOBLASTIC DISEASE

1. Signs: Beta HCG higher than expected, size-date discrepancy, hyperemesis
2. Mole Types:
   - → Complete mole- no fetal parts.
     - ✱ "Grape-like" mass or "snow-storm" on transvaginal ultrasound
   - → Incomplete mole- fetal parts.
   - → Treatment: Suction curettage
     - ✱ Risk of choriocarcinoma
     - ✱ Follow up: Monitor beta HCG weekly until undetectable
3. Choriocarcinoma- cancer of gestational contents.
   - → Treatment: Resect, methotrexate, actinomycin

REPRODUCTIVE

HYPERTENSION AND PREGNANCY

1. Treatment goal: < 140/90. Treat with Methyldopa, Hydralazine, metoprolol
    → Contraindicated: ACE inhibitors, ARBs, diuretics, calcium channel blockers
2. Pre-Eclampsia- hypertension, edema, proteinuria
3. Eclampsia- Seizures
    → Treatment: magnesium and delivery
4. HELLP syndrome- Hemolysis, elevated liver enzymes, low platelets
    → Treatment: magnesium and delivery

MULTIPLE GESTATION

1. Signs:
    → Elevated beta-HCG
    → Two or more fetuses observed on ultrasound
2. Most common complications: spontaneous abortion, preterm birth

POSTPARTUM HEMORRHAGE

1. Blood loss:
    → >500 cc for vaginal delivery
    → >1,000 cc for C. section
2. Underlying cause:
    → Boggy uterus-uterine atony
        * Treatment: Uterine massage and Pitocin
    → Absent uterus- inverted uterus
        * Treatment: Surgery
    → Firm uterus- retained placenta
        * Treatment: Surgery
    → Normal uterus- vaginal laceration or DIC
    → Unexplained-
        * Treatment: Ligate arteries.

ENDOMETRITIS

1. Presentation: Fever, uterine tenderness 2-3 days after delivery
2. Etiology: Streptococcus spp
3. Treatment: Clindamycin and Gentamicin

PREMATURE RUPTURE OF MEMBRANES

1. Most often caused by infection (E. coli)
2. Diagnosis:
    → Speculum- fluid pulling in posterior fornix
    → Nitrazine test- blue (due to elevated pH)
    → Microscope examination- ferning
3. Preterm premature rupture of membranes. <37 weeks gestation.

REPRODUCTIVE

- → >36 weeks- delivery and antibiotics (ampicillin or gentamicin)
- → >24 weeks- steroids and antibiotics

RH INCOMPATIBILITY

1. Rh negative mother, Rh positive fetus
2. Give Rho-Gam at 28 weeks, within 72 hours of delivery and during any uterine bleeding throughout pregnancy
3. Risk of hydrops fetalis.

MEDICATIONS CONTRAINDICATED IN PREGNANCY

1. Antibiotics:
   - → Quinolones, Aminoglycosides, Tetracyclines, Metronidazole
2. Antihypertensives:
   - → ACE inhibitors, ARBs, Thiazide diuretics
3. Other:
   - → Lithium, NSAIDs, thyroid medications, anticonvulsants, Warfarin

HEALTH MAINTENANCE

VACCINES

1. Birth- Hepatitis B
2. 2 months- Hepatitis B, Rotavirus, DTaP (diphtheria, tetanus, acellular pertussis), Hib (Haemophilus influenza type B), PCV (strep pneumo), IPV (inactivated polio)
3. 4 months- Rotavirus, DTaP, Hib, PCV, IPV
4. 6 months- Hepatitis B, Rotavirus, DTaP, Hib, PCV, IPV
5. 12-15 months- DTaP, Hib, PCV, IPV, Influenza, MMR, Varicella, Hepatitis A
6. 4-6 years- DTaP, IPV, MMR, Varicella
7. 11-12 years- Tdap, HPV, Meningococcal
8. 60 years- Zoster
9. 65 years- Pneumococcal polysaccharide
    → Or any time after 2 years old, if chronic illness is present
10. Other:
    → Influenza- annual
    → Tetanus booster- every 10 years or administer if open wound and no vaccination in 5 years
11. Contraindications:
    → MMR- contraindicated in pregnancy
    → Varicella- contraindicated in pregnancy and immunosuppression
    → Influenza- contraindicated if allergy to eggs or current febrile illness
    → Zoster- contraindicated if immunosuppression and gelatin or neomycin allergy
    → HPV- contraindicated in pregnancy

SCREENING TESTS

1. Newborn- TSH and PKU
2. 6-12 months- Serum lead
3. Age 21- Pap smear every 3 years until age 65
    → Age 30- pap smear and HPV every 5 years
4. Men 35, women 45, or risk factors - fasting lipid profile every 5 years.
5. Age 50 – colonoscopy every 10 years, or flexible sigmoidoscopy every 3-5 years, or fecal occult blood test every year until age 85
6. Age 50- mammogram every 2 years
7. Age 65- DEXA scan.
7. Men age 65 with history of smoking – abdominal CT for AAA

MISCELLANEOUS

1. Men over 45, postmenopausal women- Daily aspirin

CPSIA information can be obtained
at www.ICGtesting.com
Printed in the USA
BVOW05s1001150217
476017BV00002B/1/P